# Easy Desserts and Recipes in Jars - 3 Books in 1

## Over 300 Easy Recipes to Make in Jars

## Bonnie Scott

BONNIE SCOTT

ISBN-13: 978-1729519615

CONTENTS

# 100 EASY RECIPES IN JARS

# 100 MORE EASY RECIPES IN JARS 184

# DESSERTS IN JARS

BONNIE SCOTT

# 100 Easy Recipes In Jars

## Bonnie Scott

# 100 Easy Recipes In Jars

A handcrafted gift, created especially for the recipient, is truly a gift that shows how much you care. If your gift is brimming with yummy goodness, that makes it ever so much better! Create tasty and appetizing mixes for family and friends that can be used throughout the year. It's like giving love in a jar.

With recipes for everything from cookies, breads and soups to snacks and drinks, there will be a fun and festive package for everyone on your gift list this Christmas and all year long.

These recipes combine the ease of a mix with the wholesome goodness of cooking from scratch. Use the freshest and finest ingredients to make a gift that will be appreciated long after the presents are opened and the bustle of the holidays is over.

The helpful hints for assembling your creations make this project a breeze, and the colorful label and recipe templates will make your gift a colorful and memorable one.

# Filling Your Jar

Since you are using clear jars, layer the ingredients attractively. Plan the order of filling the container to make attractive contrasts of colors and textures. If your ingredients don't quite fill the jar, add extra nuts, chocolate chips or other candies that are part of the recipe for a full to the top look.

Remember that finely ground items like sugar and flour will filter down through larger items like nuts and chocolate chips, so plan the most finely ground items for the bottom layers of your sand art.

Double check the size of jar you will require to hold all the ingredients. Wide mouth jars are far easier to fill than the narrow mouth variety. One quart or one liter jars fit most recipes, but you may have to pack them tightly.

If you are adding dusty or crumbly products like cocoa, ground nuts or confectioners' sugar, wipe the inside of the jar before adding other ingredients to keep it looking clean and fresh.

Pack each layer tightly to conserve space. Use a flat-bottomed utensil or a juice glass that fits through the mouth of the jar to compress a layer before adding the next ingredient.

# Ingredients

Make sure you use the freshest ingredients, and don't scrimp by using inferior quality products. These gift jars are meant to have a fairly long shelf life, so it's important to use fresh ingredients that will last.

Tiny plastic zippered bags are inexpensive and available at the candy or jewelry center of a craft shop. If you know your jar will be sitting in storage for a while, use these to package baking soda or baking powder, as they lose their potency quickly. Tuck them in the center of the jar so they are hidden and don't ruin your sand art design.

Brown sugar hardens quickly. Package it in a plastic zipper bag or small plastic container, or make sure the recipient knows to use the mix within a few weeks, as it can become rock hard. The brown sugar can be chiseled out, but that is probably not what you want your recipient to have to do. Nuts do not have a long shelf life so be sure to purchase fresh nuts.

 If you are making up your jars ahead of time, just store them in a dry, cool, dark area and they should stay fresh. If you use fresh ingredients, the jars should be usable for up to six months.

# Decorating Your Jars

After you've packed the jars, it's time for decorating fun. Choose colors that will coordinate with the recipient's kitchen décor, or select colors to celebrate the season.

Scraps of patterned fabrics are inexpensive and you only need a small square or two to cover your jar lid. Use pinking shears to make a zigzag border for a country look. If you use a loosely woven fabric, unravel the edges to create fringe for a shabby chic look. Two squares of fabric, turned 90 degrees from each other, gives a double punch of color.

Use a thin rubber band to secure the fabric in place on the lid. You can now fuss with your fabric to get the positioning just right before adding the ribbon, which will cover the rubber band.

Use ribbon, twine or a leather cord to tie around your jar lid. Natural or paper raffia is also available at local craft shops and available in many colors. Use your pinking shears to cut narrow strips of fabric to use as your ribbon, or use rickrack or lace to tie up your gift.

You can also use bits of lace, rick rack or other festive trims and buttons to add texture and color. Your glue stick is your friend and it's easy to add fun embellishments to give your gift a designer look. Double sided tape can also easily adhere your trim to the container.

Add custom labels, hang tags and recipe cards to your gifts. You can customize them with personal messages, or create generic tags that can be used for any occasion. Use a hole punch to make a hole to hang your tag with string or ribbon.

# Other Fun Filled Containers

There are lots of other options for decorative gift containers. Use a heavy duty plastic freezer bag to hold all the ingredients, and pop them in a decorative tin container or cookie jar. Bundle the bag up in colorful cellophane and tie with a bow. Add it to a basket lined with a kitchen towel. You can also sew a cloth drawstring bag in holiday fabric to hold your gift, and tie it up with a bit of holly and your hanging gift tag. Jars are heavy for mailing, so the plastic freezer bag is a great alternative for sending cookie mix to relatives.

Get the kids involved. Buy inexpensive cardboard gift containers at a local craft shop, or save lidded oatmeal containers. Let the children paint and decoupage the outside of the gift boxes, then fill with a bagged mix. You can add your own label and recipe card to their masterpiece.

For a new bride or a young person setting up their first kitchen, place your cellophane, ribbon decorated gift in a great mixing bowl. Add a wooden spoon with a bow to complete the gift. To make a complete baking set, include a cookie sheet, timer, measuring cup and spoons.

Tie a set of cookie cutters with a ribbon, and attach it to a sugar cookie mix jar. For a family gift, wrap your cookie mix jar in a kitchen towel to protect the glass. Place it in a festive new cookie jar. Mom will appreciate the new canister and towel, while the kids enjoy the fresh baked cookies.


Other ideas for cookie gift jars might include pairing cookie mix and cocoa mix jars in a basket with a small bag of mini-marshmallows. Add a family favorite DVD movie for a perfect evening at home gift.

Dip the bowl ends of plastic spoons in melted chocolate.

Scatter with colored sugar or candy sprinkles, and tie up one or two in a piece of cellophane. Attach to a gift jar of cocoa or flavored coffee mix with a decorative ribbon.

Another taste treat to add to a beverage mix is homemade biscotti. Dip one end in melted chocolate chips or chocolate bark. Tie up a nice selection with cellophane and attach to your gift jar.

Add a jar of cocoa or coffee mix, a pair of cute ceramic mugs and a holiday CD to a gift basket. You could purchase a small serving tray, tie the entire set in cellophane and add a big bow to the top.

# Other Recipe In A Jar Uses

Recipes in a jar are great items for fund raising. Use them for silent auctions, raffles, church bazaars and craft shows.

If your child's school has a Santa's Store for students to buy gifts for their parents and relatives, recipes in a jar are great ideas for kids to purchase as Christmas gifts.

Jars that are being sold should have generic gift tags and labels so the giver can personalize them.

These ready-to-use jars also make great emergency gifts for unexpected guests and last-minute additions to your gift-giving list.

A mix in a jar is also a thoughtful 'welcome to the neighborhood' present for a new neighbor.

Jars are also popular as wedding favors or wedding table decorations. Personalize the jars with the names of your guests and show off your creative side at the same time.

Wedding favor jars are popular and help hold down the cost of a wedding. Have a cute personalized label professionally printed with the names and wedding date.

# Hints And Tips

Fill jars to the top to eliminate as much air as possible and to avoid the possibility of disturbing the layers when the jar is moved.

If the ingredients are packaged in a plastic bag, squeeze out as much air as possible before sealing it. This will help to keep the contents fresh.

Place the finest ground ingredients at the bottom of the jar. This includes items like sugar, flour and confectioners sugar. If placed above coarse items like nuts or chocolate chips they will seep down through the layers, and your gift will not retain its sand art look.

Store gift jars in a cool, dark and dry area. The ingredients will remain usable up to six months, provided the ingredients are fresh. Placing the jar for display on a sunny windowsill or counter will significantly reduce the shelf life of your mix.

You should package baking powder and baking soda separately in sealed bags to ensure freshness, if the jar will not be used right away.

Mark your gift with the giving date. The recipient won't have to worry about the ingredients becoming stale if they know the date the jar originated.

# Putting the Jars Together

## STEP BY STEP

# Fabric Top

I like using 2 pieces of fabric on the top of quart jars, but just one piece also works nicely. I use from a 6" square to a 9" square. Use a 6 or 6 1/2" square or even smaller if you want the top layer in your jar to be viewable. I even use a 6" square for the smaller half-pint jars. In the cover photo, the red and green dotted fabrics are 6" squares. One square in the red dotted fabric, one in the green dotted fabric, placed at angles to each other. The M&M's® layer shows up nicely with the shorter fabric.

The red dot fabric on the cover is a 6 1/2" square. The red dot fabric combined with the white fabric hang nice but farther from the top of the jar by being just 1/2" longer.

The brown and teal fabrics on the cover are 9" squares. They create a more dramatic cover on the top of the jar. This longer top dresses up the jar when you don't have anything especially colorful to show off in the jar (like M&M's®) or when the whole jar is mixed up anyway, as with some of the snacks.

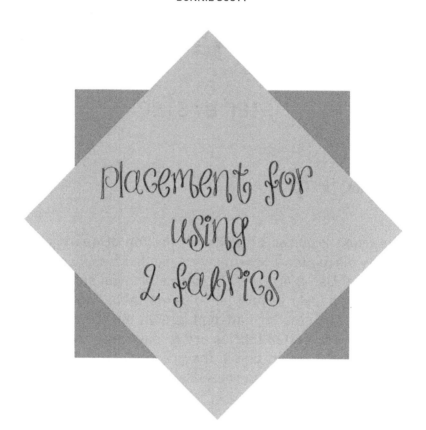

Placement for using 2 fabrics

# Ribbon and Decorative Trim

I use a thin rubber band about 3" long around the top of the jar over the fabric before adding the ribbon or trim. The thin, loose rubber band will allow the fabric to be manipulated and straightened before applying the trim, yet hold the fabric in place.

Thin ribbons work best, but if they are too thin, the rubber band may show through. 3/8" ribbon is what I use on most of the jars. 1/8" decorative trim does look pretty but may show some of the rubber band. Use approximately 30 inches of ribbon for each top.

Thin lengths of jute also look cute, especially on homespun fabrics. Raffia is another medium that can be used for the bow.

Some jars in this book do not actually have fabric adorning the top, but just have decorative trim wound around the lid. Double sided tape works great for holding the trim in place if just a few pieces of tape are placed on the jar lid rim before winding the trim around.

All the ribbons, trim and fabrics used in this book are available at either Hobby Lobby stores or Joann fabric stores.

# Labels, Hang Tags, Recipe Cards

Each recipe in this book has 3 pages of labels, tags and recipe cards available to print out. Since there are 100 recipes, there are 300 pages of labels, way too many to include in this book. So the labels are available on the internet and can be accessed with your computer and printed.

There is a large variety of holiday labels, everyday labels and recipe cards. Also the jars are available for viewing on the web page in color.

Ideas for attaching the recipe cards to the jars:

- Attach to the jar fabric or ribbon with a safety pin
- Punch a hole in the recipe card and tie it to the ribbon with jute or ribbon
- Roll the recipe card up like a scroll and tie it with jute or ribbon

- If the recipe is short and sweet, just print out the small recipe card and stick it to the back of the jar. I have made printable labels just for that purpose when the recipe is brief.

Access this books recipe labels, tags and recipe cards at:

# www.NorthPoleChristmas.com/jars.html

# Visual Jar Filling

Putting the ingredients in a jar:

Supplies that are not necessary but make jarring a whole lot easier if you are making more than one or two jars are:

- canning funnel

- bean masher or other utensil that is flat on the bottom with a handle

The canning jars are available at Walmart and canning funnels are stocked by the jars.

Approximately 4 3/4 cups will fit in a quart jar if it is packed tightly and 4 cups if it cannot be packed as with nuts. 2 cups of snacks (unpacked) will fit in a pint jar.

The following pages are the basic steps you will go through in filling a jar. The jar I am filling in the examples is for the Holiday Cranberry Cookies.

Start by placing the funnel over the jar.

Next the flour mixture is usually added. It is the messiest layer and the flour will seep through any other layer (like raisins) that you cannot pack tightly, so I normally place it first in the jar.

Pack the flour mixture with the bean masher. The flour may make a mess on the inside of the jar and if it does, after packing the flour, just use a paper towel and clean the inside of the jar.

Next a packable layer like the brown sugar is nice to add. It keeps the flour where it is supposed to be in the jar.

Now pack the brown sugar firmly.

My bean masher actually has a scalloped pattern on the edge and sometimes I get that cute pattern on the brown sugar edge.

Next I added the white sugar.

Pack the sugar layer firmly. Just pack each layer as you go unless the layer is an ingredient like chocolate chips. Even the chip layer can be pushed down lightly.

Dried cranberries are added next. They can be packed a little, but don't pack too hard. You don't want cranberry juice in the jar.

Last in this recipe to add are vanilla chips. They will sit loosely on top of everything else in the jar. It is smart to put nuts, chips or fruit as the final layer, in case your packing was not as firm as you thought and you run out of room. You can always put just a little less of those ingredients in the jar or add more if you have the room.

And voilà, the final jar is ready for sealing and decorating. For sealing, just be sure the metal lid is clean, especially the rubber coating along the edge. Clean the top rim of the jar before placing the lid on, then add the ring and tighten. This is not actually a sealing process as in canning but will keep your ingredients fresh for quite a while.

The final finished project – Holiday Cranberry Cookies

# Cookies

Most of the cookie recipes yield about 24 cookies, give or take a few depending on the ingredients in the jar and the size of the cookie.

## Kris Kringle Granola Cookies

1 1/4 cups all-purpose flour
3/4 teaspoon salt
3/4 teaspoon baking soda
1/2 cup granulated sugar
1/2 cup packed brown sugar
1 1/4 cups granola
1/2 cup chocolate chips
1/2 cup M & M's
1/4 cup walnuts
Jar – Wide mouth quart glass canning jar

Combine flour, salt and baking soda. Layer in jar in this order: flour mixture, granola, brown sugar, granulated sugar, M&M's, chocolate chips and finally, walnuts. Pack each layer. Seal jar.

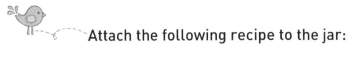Attach the following recipe to the jar:

Kris Kringle Granola Cookies

2/3 cup margarine, softened
3/4 teaspoon vanilla
1 egg

Preheat oven to 350 degrees F. Combine margarine, vanilla and egg in a bowl. Add the cookie mix from the jar to bowl and stir until well blended. Line a cookie sheet with parchment paper or use ungreased cookie sheet. Drop dough by rounded spoonfuls and bake for 10 to 12 minutes. Makes 2 dozen cookies.

# Santa's M&M Cookie Mix

2 cups all-purpose flour
1 teaspoon baking soda
1 teaspoon baking powder
1 teaspoon salt
1 cup brown sugar (not packed)
1/2 cup granulated sugar
1 1/4 cups M&M's candies
Jar – Wide mouth quart glass canning jar

Mix flour with baking soda, baking powder and salt. Layer ingredients in the jar in this order: flour mixture, brown sugar, granulated sugar, M&M's. Pack each layer firmly in jar so all the ingredients will fit. Be sure to put the M&M's on top so they can be separated for the recipe below.

 Attach the following recipe to the jar:

Santa's M&M Cookies

1 cup margarine, softened
2 eggs
2 teaspoons vanilla

Preheat oven to 350 degrees F. Mix vanilla, margarine and eggs in a large bowl. Set aside half of the M&M's in the cookie mix jar. Pour the rest of the jar mixture into a large bowl and stir until mixed. Add margarine mixture to cookie mix and stir until completely blended. (Be sure margarine is cooled before adding the M&M's.)

Lightly grease a cookie sheet. Drop dough by spoonfuls on cookie sheet and push a few M&M's on top of each cookie. Bake for 9 to 10 minutes until cookies are just golden brown on the edges. Makes 3 dozen cookies.

# Cinnamon Oatmeal Cookie Mix

3/4 cup all-purpose flour
1/4 teaspoon baking soda
1 1/4 teaspoons cinnamon
1/2 teaspoon salt
2/3 cup packed brown sugar
1/4 cup granulated sugar
1 3/4 cups quick cooking oats
1/2 cup chopped walnuts
Jar – Wide mouth quart glass canning jar

Mix together flour, baking soda, salt and cinnamon. In the jar, place flour mixture and pack, then add the rest of the ingredients on top.

Attach the following recipe to the jar:

Cinnamon Oatmeal Cookies

1/2 cup butter, softened
1 egg
1 1/4 teaspoon vanilla extract

Preheat oven to 325 degrees F. In a large bowl, mix together butter, egg and vanilla. Pour mixture from the jar into the bowl; mix well. Drop dough by spoonfuls on ungreased cookie sheet. Bake for 12 minutes.

# Dark Chocolate Chunk Cookie Mix

*These are absolutely the best cookies for any dark chocolate lover. The recipe below will fill a quart jar to the brim, so be sure to pack each layer well, even the chocolate.*

1 3/4 cups all-purpose flour
1/4 teaspoon salt
1 teaspoon baking powder
1 teaspoon baking soda
1/2 cup cocoa powder
7 ounces dark chocolate (1 giant candy bar or 2 regular candy bars)
3/4 cup brown sugar
1/2 cup granulated sugar
Jar – Wide mouth quart glass canning jar

Break chocolate bars into chunks. Mix together flour, salt, baking powder and baking soda. Layer the ingredients in the jar in this order: flour mixture, dark chocolate chunks, brown sugar, cocoa powder, granulated sugar. Pack each layer firmly in jar.

Attach the following recipe to the jar:

Dark Chocolate Chunk Cookies

3/4 cup soft margarine
1 egg, slightly beaten
2 teaspoons vanilla

Preheat oven to 350 degrees F. Mix egg, margarine and vanilla in a large bowl. Empty the jar of cookie mix into bowl. Stir until well blended. Line a baking sheet with parchment paper or lightly grease. Drop dough by spoonful on baking sheet and bake for 9 to 11 minutes until just golden brown on the edges. Makes 4 dozen cookies.

Dark Chocolate Chunk Cookies

# Chewy Raisin Cookie Mix

1 cup all-purpose flour
1/2 teaspoon ground nutmeg
3/4 teaspoon ground cinnamon
1/2 teaspoon salt
3/4 teaspoon baking soda
1 cup packed brown sugar
1/2 cup raisins
2 1/4 cups rolled oats
Jar – Wide mouth quart glass canning jar

Add salt, cinnamon, nutmeg and baking soda to flour and mix. In the jar, layer flour mixture, sugar, oats and finally, the raisins on top, being sure to pack each layer except the raisins.

 Attach the following recipe to the jar:

Chewy Raisin Cookies

3/4 cup margarine, softened
1 egg, slightly beaten
1 teaspoon of vanilla
2 teaspoons of honey

Preheat oven to 350 degrees F. Mix butter, egg, honey and vanilla in a large bowl. Add contents of the jar to the bowl. Stir until well blended. Drop by spoonfuls on a lightly greased cookie sheet. Bake 10 to 14 minutes or until cookies begin to brown.

# Chocolate Cherry Cookie Mix

1 1/2 cups all-purpose flour
1/8 teaspoon salt
1/2 cup brown sugar
1 1/2 cup chocolate chips
Small jar of maraschino cherries (about 24)
Jar - 1 wide mouth quart canning jar

Mix flour and salt together. Layer flour mixture, brown sugar, then chocolate chips in the jar. Be sure to put the chocolate chips on top so they can be used separately in the recipe below. Give the jar of cherries along with the quart canning jar.

Attach the following recipe to the jar:

Chocolate Cherry Cookies

1/2 cup margarine
1 teaspoon vanilla

Preheat oven to 350 degrees F. Remove the chocolate chips from the jar and set aside. Mix vanilla and margarine together. Add the rest of the dry ingredients from the jar (all except the chocolate chips) and mix well.

Drain the jar of maraschino cherries. Put a chocolate chip inside each cherry, then wrap about a teaspoon of dough around the cherry. Bake on an ungreased cookie sheet for 12 to 15 minutes. Melt the remainder of the chocolate chips in the microwave and dip the top of cookies in the melted chocolate.

# Oatmeal Chocolate Chip Cookie Mix

1 cup all-purpose flour
1/4 teaspoon salt
1/2 teaspoon baking soda
1/2 teaspoon cinnamon
1/2 cup packed brown sugar
1/4 cup granulated sugar
1 1/4 cups rolled oats
1 cup semi-sweet chocolate chips
2/3 cup chopped walnuts

Jar – Wide mouth quart glass canning jar

Mix flour, salt, cinnamon and baking soda together. Layer in the jar - flour mixture, sugars, oats and chocolate chips and walnuts on top.

Attach the following recipe to the jar:

Oatmeal Chocolate Chip Cookies

1 egg
1/2 cup butter, softened
1 teaspoon vanilla extract

Preheat oven to 350 degrees F. Cream butter, egg and vanilla in a large bowl. Empty the jar of cookie mix into the bowl. Stir until well blended. Drop by spoonfuls on an ungreased cookie sheet. Bake 9 to 10 minutes or until light brown.

# Gingerbread Cookie Mix

*Tie one or more cookie cutters to the jar for this recipe.*

3 1/2 cups all-purpose flour
1/2 teaspoon salt
1 teaspoon baking soda
1 teaspoon ground ginger
1/2 teaspoon ground allspice
1/2 teaspoon ground cinnamon
1/2 teaspoon ground cloves
1/2 cup packed brown sugar
Gingerbread boy cookie cutter
Jar – Wide mouth quart glass canning jar

Mix all the spices, baking soda and flour. Layer flour mixture in the jar, then brown sugar, packing each layer.

 Attach the following recipe to the jar:

Gingerbread Cookies

3/4 cup dark molasses
3 tablespoons shortening
1/3 cup cold water
Can of chocolate or vanilla frosting

Mix together molasses, water and shortening in a large bowl. Empty jar of cookie mix into the bowl and stir until well blended. Cover and refrigerate for 1 hour or longer. Preheat oven to 350 degrees F. Roll dough to 1/4" thick on a lightly floured surface. Cut into shapes with cookie cutter.

Lightly grease a baking sheet and bake 10 to 15 minutes. Decorate with icing.

Gingerbread Cookies

# Santa's Sugar Cookie Mix

*This is another jar that would be cute with cookie cutters added to your ribbon or bow.*

3 cups all-purpose flour
1 teaspoon baking powder
1/2 teaspoon salt
1 1/2 cup granulated sugar
Jar - 1 wide mouth quart canning jar

Mix flour, baking powder and salt together. Layer the flour mixture, then sugar in the jar. Be sure to add sugar as the last layer so it can be separated for the recipe below.

Attach the following recipe to the jar:

Santa's Sugar Cookies

1 cup margarine, softened
3 eggs
2 teaspoons vanilla extract

Preheat oven to 375 degrees F. Pour top sugar layer from the jar into a large bowl. Add margarine and cream until smooth. Add vanilla and eggs and stir well. Stir in the rest of the mixture from the jar. Refrigerate dough for one hour or overnight. Roll the cold dough thinly on parchment paper or a floured surface. Cut with cookie cutters and bake on ungreased cookie sheet for 6 to 8 minutes or until lightly golden in color.

Tip: Roll the dough out on parchment paper, then use cookie cutters to cut the shapes. Just remove the excess dough from around the cutouts. Then the parchment paper is ready to slide onto a cookie sheet to bake.

Santa's Sugar Cookies

# Chocolate Chip Cookie Mix

1 teaspoon salt
1 teaspoon baking soda
2 cups all-purpose flour
3/4 cup brown sugar, packed
3/4 cup granulated sugar
1 1/4 cups semi-sweet chocolate chips
Jar – Wide mouth quart glass canning jar

Mix flour, salt and baking soda together, then layer flour mixture, sugars and chocolate chips on top, being sure to pack each layer firmly.

 Attach the following recipe to the jar:

Chocolate Chip Cookies

1 cup butter, softened
2 eggs
1 teaspoon vanilla
Optional – 1 cup chopped nuts

Preheat oven to 375 degrees F. Cream butter, eggs and vanilla in a large bowl. Empty the jar of cookie mix into the bowl. Stir until well blended. Lightly grease a baking sheet. Bake 8 to 10 minutes.

# Peanut Butter Chunk Cookie Mix

1 3/4 cups all-purpose flour
1 teaspoon baking soda
1/2 teaspoon salt
1/2 cup granulated sugar
1/2 cup packed brown sugar
8 Reese's peanut butter cups cut into 1/2" pieces
Jar – Wide mouth quart glass canning jar

Mix together flour, salt and baking soda. Layer the ingredients in the jar - flour mixture, brown sugar, granulated sugar, peanut butter cup pieces.

Attach the following recipe to the jar:

Peanut Butter Chunk Cookies

1 egg, slightly beaten
1 teaspoon vanilla
1/2 cup margarine, softened
1/2 cup peanut butter

Preheat oven to 375 degrees F. Remove peanut butter cups from the jar. Empty the rest of the cookie mix into a large mixing bowl and stir until well blended. Add margarine, egg, peanut butter and vanilla to the mix and stir well. Add the peanut butter cups.

Shape into 1" balls or use a small cookie scoop. Bake for 8 to 10 minutes until cookies are just golden brown on the edges. Makes 2 1/2 dozen cookies.

# Holiday Cranberry Cookie Mix

1 3/4 cups all-purpose flour
1/2 teaspoon baking soda
1/2 cup brown sugar, packed
1/2 cup granulated sugar
1 cup dried cranberries
3/4 cup white chocolate baking chips
Jar – Wide mouth quart glass canning jar

Mix the flour and baking soda together. Layer in the jar - flour mixture, brown sugar, sugar, cranberries and white chips. Pack each layer well. Seal jar.

Attach the following recipe to the jar:

Holiday Cranberry Cookies

1 egg
1 teaspoon vanilla
1/2 cup margarine, softened

Preheat oven to 375 degrees F. Mix together the egg, vanilla and margarine in a large bowl. Add the contents of the jar and mix well. Lightly grease a cookie sheet. Drop by heaping spoonfuls on cookie sheet. Bake for 8 to 10 minutes.

# Chocolate Covered Banana Cookie Mix

2 cups all-purpose flour
1/4 teaspoon baking soda
1/2 teaspoon salt
1 teaspoon baking powder
1/2 cup brown sugar, packed
1/4 cup white sugar
2 cups semi-sweet chocolate chips
Jar – Wide mouth quart glass canning jar

Mix together the flour, baking soda, salt and baking powder. In the jar, layer the flour mixture, brown sugar, white sugar, then the chocolate chips, packing each layer. Seal the jar.

Attach the following recipe to the jar:

Chocolate Covered Banana Cookies

1/2 cup butter, softened
2 eggs
1 teaspoon vanilla extract
1 cup ripe bananas, mashed

Preheat oven to 400 degrees F. Mix the butter, eggs and vanilla. Add the mashed bananas. Next add the contents of the jar and stir until well mixed. Drop by spoonfuls on greased cookie sheets. Bake for 12 to 15 minutes.

# Vanilla Chip Cookie Mix

1 cup all-purpose flour
1/4 teaspoon salt
1/2 teaspoon baking soda
1/2 cup sugar
1/4 cup brown sugar, packed
1 cup white chocolate chips
1/2 cup flaked coconut
1 cup Macadamia nuts, chopped
Jar - 1 wide mouth quart canning jar

Mix the flour, baking soda and salt together. Layer the flour mixture, brown sugar, white sugar, coconut, nuts and white chocolate chips in the jar. Seal jar.

Attach the following recipe to the jar:

Vanilla Chip Cookies

1/2 cup margarine, softened
1 teaspoon vanilla
1 egg

Preheat oven to 375 degrees F. Mix together the margarine, vanilla and egg. Add the contents of the jar and stir well. Drop by spoonfuls onto ungreased cookie sheets. Bake for 12 minutes or until golden.

# Krispies Cookie Mix

1 3/4 cups all-purpose flour
1/2 teaspoon salt
1/2 teaspoon cream of tartar
1/2 teaspoon baking soda
1/2 cup granulated sugar
1/2 cup brown sugar
1/2 cup Rice Krispies
1/2 cup oatmeal
1/2 cup coconut
1/4 cup chopped walnuts
Jar – Wide mouth quart glass canning jar

Mix the flour, salt, cream of tartar and baking soda together in a bowl. Place the flour mixture in a jar, then the brown sugar and white sugar and add the rest of the ingredients in any order. Seal jar.

Attach the following recipe to the jar:

Krispies Cookies

1 cup margarine
1 cup corn oil or vegetable oil
2 eggs
1 teaspoon vanilla

Preheat oven to 350 degrees F. Mix together the eggs, margarine, oil and vanilla. Add the ingredients from the jar and mix well. Drop by tablespoonful's on ungreased cookie sheet. Bake for 12 minutes - don't brown.

# Snickerdoodles Cookie Mix

2 3/4 cups all-purpose flour
1/4 teaspoon salt
1 teaspoon baking soda
2 teaspoons cream of tartar
1 1/2 cups white sugar
Jar – Wide mouth quart glass canning jar

Combine the flour, salt, cream of tartar and baking soda. Pack the flour mixture in the jar and add the sugar on top. Seal jar.

Attach the following recipe to the jar:

Snickerdoodle Cookies

1 cup margarine or butter
2 eggs
2 tablespoons white sugar
2 teaspoons cinnamon

Preheat oven to 400 degrees F. In a large bowl, mix together the butter and eggs. Add the contents of the jar to the bowl and mix well. In a separate bowl, mix together the white sugar and cinnamon. Shape the dough into 1 1/2" balls and then roll the balls in the cinnamon sugar. Bake for 8 to 10 minutes, until lightly brown.

Snickerdoodle Cookies

# Chocolate Coconut Cookie Mix

3/4 cup all-purpose flour
1/4 teaspoon salt
1/2 teaspoon baking soda
1/2 cup packed brown sugar
1/4 cup white sugar
1 1/2 cups rolled oats
1 cup semi-sweet chocolate chips
1/2 cup shredded coconut
Jar – Wide mouth quart glass canning jar

Mix the flour, salt and baking soda together. In a jar, layer the flour mixture, brown sugar, white sugar, oats, chocolate chips and coconut, packing each layer. Seal the jar.

 Attach the following recipe to the jar:

Chocolate Coconut Cookies

1/2 cup butter, softened
1 egg
1 tablespoon milk
1 teaspoon vanilla extract

Preheat oven to 350 degrees F. Mix together the butter, egg, milk and vanilla. Add the cookie mix from the jar and stir until well blended. Drop by spoonfuls on greased cookie sheets. Bake for 7 to 10 minutes.

# Chocolate Dreams Cookie Mix

1 package brownie mix (19.8 ounces)
1/4 cup all-purpose flour
2 cups peanut butter chips
Jar – Wide mouth quart glass canning jar

In the jar, layer the brownie mix, flour and peanut butter chips, packing each layer. Seal the jar.

Attach the following recipe to the jar:

Chocolate Dreams Cookies

2 eggs
3 tablespoons water
1/4 cup vegetable oil

Preheat oven to 350 degrees F. In a medium bowl, combine the eggs, water and vegetable oil. Add the jar of cookie mix and stir until blended. Lightly grease a cookie sheet. Drop dough by the spoonful on the cookie sheet and bake for 8 to 9 minutes. Makes 2 dozen.

# Noel Toffee Cookie Mix

1 1/2 cups all-purpose flour
1/2 teaspoon baking soda
1/2 teaspoon salt
3/4 cup brown sugar, packed
1 1/2 cup toffee baking bits (or Heath toffee bits)
1/2 cup semi-sweet chocolate chips
1/2 cup chopped walnuts or pecans
Jar – Wide mouth quart glass canning jar

Combine the flour, salt and baking soda. Layer in jar - flour mixture, brown sugar, toffee baking bits, chocolate chips and nuts. Pack each layer well and seal jar.

Attach the following recipe to the jar:

Noel Toffee Cookies

1/2 cup margarine
1 egg
1 teaspoon vanilla extract

Preheat oven to 350 degrees F. In a large bowl, mix margarine, egg, and vanilla. Add the contents of the jar and mix well. Drop by spoonfuls on a lightly greased cookie sheet. Press down on each cookie a bit. Bake about 12 to 15 minutes. Makes 18 cookies.

# Oatmeal M&M Cookie Mix

2 1/3 cups rolled oats
1 teaspoon baking soda
1/4 cup M&M's®
1/3 cup semi-sweet chocolate chips
1/2 cup white sugar
2/3 cup packed brown sugar
Jar – Wide mouth quart glass canning jar

Mix the oats and baking soda together and put in jar. Pack down firmly. Add the rest of the ingredients in this order - M&M's®, chocolate chips, brown sugar and white sugar. Seal jar.

Attach the following recipe to the jar:

Oatmeal M&M Cookies

1/4 cup butter or margarine
1/4 teaspoon vanilla
2 eggs
2/3 cup peanut butter

Preheat oven to 350 degrees F. In a large bowl, mix together butter, vanilla, eggs and peanut butter. Add all the ingredients from the jar. Shape dough into 1" balls. Bake on a lightly greased cookie sheet for 10 to 12 minutes.

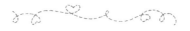

# Crunchy Cookie Mix

1 1/4 cup all-purpose flour
1/2 teaspoon baking soda
1/2 teaspoon baking powder
1 cup oatmeal
1/2 cup white sugar
1/2 cup brown sugar, packed
3/4 cup corn flakes
1/4 cup coconut
1/2 cup salted peanuts
Jar – Wide mouth quart glass canning jar

Mix the flour, baking powder and baking soda together. In the jar, layer the flour mixture, then all the rest of the ingredients. Seal the jar.

 Attach the following recipe to the jar:

Crunchy Cookies

1 egg
1/2 teaspoon vanilla
3/4 cup margarine, melted

Preheat oven to 350 degrees F. Mix together the egg, vanilla and margarine in a large bowl. Add the contents of the jar and mix well. Drop by spoonfuls on an ungreased cookie sheet. Bake for 8 to 10 minutes.

# Cappuccino Noel Balls Mix

1 3/4 cups all-purpose flour
1/2 teaspoon salt
1/4 cup unsweetened cocoa powder
1 tablespoon instant coffee granules
1/2 cup white sugar
2 cups finely chopped pecans
Jar - wide mouth quart canning jar

Stir together the flour, salt, cocoa powder and instant coffee. Layer in jar: flour mixture, sugar and pecans.

 Attach the following recipe to the jar:

Cappuccino Noel Balls

1 cup butter softened
2 teaspoons vanilla extract
1 cup confectioners' sugar for rolling

Preheat the oven to 325 degrees F. In a large bowl, stir together the butter and vanilla until well mixed. Mix in the ingredients from the jar and stir until mixed. Roll the dough into 1 inch balls and bake on a lightly greased cookie sheet. Bake for 15 to 20 minutes until the bottoms are lightly browned. Remove from cookie sheet and while warm, roll in the confectioners' sugar.

# Bakery Style Chocolate Chip Cookies

1 1/2 cups all-purpose flour
1/2 teaspoon salt
1/4 teaspoon cinnamon
1/2 teaspoon baking soda
3/4 cup brown sugar, packed
1/3 cup granulated sugar
1 1/2 cups semi-sweet chocolate chips
Jar – Wide mouth quart glass canning jar

Mix flour, salt, cinnamon and baking soda together and put in jar. Pack down firmly. Add chocolate chips, brown sugar and granulated sugar in layers. Put the sugars on top so they can be removed separately for the recipe. Seal jar.

Attach the following recipe to the jar:

Bakery Style Chocolate Chip Cookies

2 1/4 teaspoons vanilla extract
1 egg
1 egg yolk
1/2 cup butter, melted

Preheat oven to 325 degrees F. Remove granulated sugar and brown sugar from the jar (top 2 layers) and place in a large bowl. Add melted butter to  sugars and stir until well mixed. Add egg, egg yolk and vanilla and mix well until light and creamy. Mix in the rest of the contents of the jar. Place cookie dough by spoonfuls on a cookie sheet and flatten cookies a bit. Bake cookies for 15 to 16 minutes or until edges are turning light brown.

# Craisin Cookie Mix

2 cups all-purpose flour
1 teaspoon ground cinnamon
1 1/4 teaspoons baking soda
1 1/3 cups packed brown sugar
1 cup Craisins
Jar - wide mouth quart canning jar

Mix flour, cinnamon and baking soda together. Layer in jar: flour mixture, brown sugar and Craisins. Seal jar.

Attach the following recipe to the jar:

Craisin Cookies

2/3 cup margarine
1 egg
1/2 cup milk

Preheat oven to 350 degrees F. In a large bowl, stir together margarine and milk, then add egg. Add the contents of the jar. Stir well. Drop dough by rounded spoonfuls on an ungreased cookie sheet. Bake for 10 to 12 minutes.

# Sugar Cookie Mix

*This cookie mix will fit in a pint jar.*

2 cups all-purpose flour
1/2 teaspoon ground cloves
1/2 teaspoon ginger
2 teaspoons baking soda
1/2 teaspoon salt
1 teaspoon cinnamon
Jar – Wide mouth pint glass canning jar

Mix together all ingredients above. Put in jar and seal.

 Attach the following recipe to the jar:

Sugar Cookies

3/4 cup soft margarine
1 cup granulated sugar
1/4 cup molasses
1 egg
Extra granulated sugar for rolling

Mix together margarine, granulated sugar, molasses and egg, and beat well. Add the contents of the jar. Stir until well blended and chill for 1 hour or overnight.

Preheat oven to 375 degrees F. Form cold dough into balls and roll cookies in sugar. (Can also be rolled in Christmas sprinkles for a more festive look.) Place on greased cookie sheet. Bake for 8 to10 minutes.

# Magical Caramel Cookie Mix

1 1/3 cups all-purpose flour
1/2 teaspoon baking soda
1/2 cup granulated sugar
1/3 cup baking cocoa
1/2 cup brown sugar, packed
1/2 package Rolo candies or Hershey's Caramel Kisses (about 24)
Jar – Wide mouth quart glass canning jar

Combine flour and baking soda. Layer in jar in this order: flour mixture, cocoa, granulated sugar, brown sugar, candies. Pack each layer well except for candies and seal jar.

 Attach the following recipe to the jar:

Magical Caramel Cookies

1/2 cup margarine, softened
1 egg
1 1/2 teaspoons vanilla
Sugar for rolling cookies in

Preheat oven to 375 degrees F. Remove candies from the jar, unwrap each one and set aside. In a large bowl, combine egg, margarine and vanilla. Add the rest of the contents of the jar to the bowl and stir well. Using about a tablespoon of dough, shape it around each candy covering the candy completely, then roll the dough in granulated

sugar. Place on an ungreased cookie sheet. Bake for 7 to 10 minutes or until top is barely cracked. Makes 24 cookies.
sugar. Place on an ungreased cookie sheet. Bake for 7 to 10 minutes or until top is barely cracked. Makes 24 cookies.

# Chocolate Mint Cookie Mix

2 cups all-purpose flour
1 1/2 teaspoons baking powder
1/2 teaspoon salt
2 tablespoons cocoa
1 cup granulated sugar
1/4 cup mint-chocolate chips
1/4 cup pecans, chopped
Jar – Wide mouth quart glass canning jar

Mix flour, baking powder, salt and cocoa together. In the jar, layer the flour mixture, then all the rest of the ingredients. Seal the jar.

Attach the following recipe to the jar:

Chocolate Mint Cookies

1 egg, beaten
1 teaspoon vanilla
2 tablespoons milk
1/2 cup margarine or shortening, melted

Preheat oven to 350 degrees F. Mix together egg, vanilla, milk and margarine in a large bowl. Add the contents of the jar and mix well. Drop by spoonfuls on a lightly greased cookie sheet. Bake for 8 to 10 minutes.

# Mrs. Kringle's Chocolate Kiss Cookie Mix

1 3/4 cup all-purpose flour
1/4 teaspoon salt
3/4 teaspoon baking soda
1 1/2 cup granulated sugar
1/2 cup unsweetened cocoa powder
About 20 chocolate kisses
Jar – Wide mouth quart glass canning jar

Combine flour, salt and baking soda. Layer in jar as follows: flour mixture, cocoa powder, sugar, chocolate kisses.

Attach the following recipe to the jar:

Mrs. Kringle's Chocolate Kiss Cookies

3/4 cup butter, softened
2 eggs
1 1/2 teaspoon vanilla
Granulated sugar

Preheat oven to 350 degrees F. Unwrap chocolate kisses. Mix together butter, eggs and vanilla. Add the contents of the jar and mix well. Form a tablespoon of dough into a 1" ball. Roll in sugar. Place on an ungreased cookie sheet and bake for 8 to10 minutes. Place chocolate kiss in the middle of each cookie while still hot.

# Thumbprint Cookie Mix

1/2 cup granulated sugar
2 1/4 cups all-purpose flour
3/4 teaspoon salt
1 1/2 cups finely chopped walnuts
Jar – Wide mouth quart glass canning jar

Mix flour and salt together. In the jar, layer flour mixture, granulated sugar and walnuts on top. Be sure to put the nuts on top because they will need to be removed and set aside when baking. Seal the jar.

Attach the following recipe to the jar:

Thumbprint Cookies

1 1/2 teaspoons vanilla
3 eggs
1 cup butter or margarine
1/2 cup strawberry, grape or apricot preserves

Preheat oven to 350 degrees F. Remove walnuts from the top layer of the jar and set aside. Separate eggs into 2 bowls – 3 egg yolks in one and 3 egg whites in the other. In a large bowl, mix butter, egg yolks and vanilla together. Add the rest of the ingredients from the jar and mix well. Shape cookies into small balls about 3/4". Dip each one in the egg whites and then roll it in nuts. Place on a lightly greased cookie sheet and press down on each cookie with your thumb. Bake for 15 to 17 minutes. Fill thumbprints on the cookie with preserves when cool.

# Popcorn Seasoning

## Cheesy Popcorn Spice Mix

1/2 cup grated parmesan cheese
2 teaspoons salt
1 teaspoon dried tarragon
1 teaspoon parsley flakes
1 teaspoon garlic powder
Jar – Wide mouth half-pint glass canning jar

Combine all ingredients in a small bowl; stir until well blended. Put in a half-pint jar.

 Attach the following recipe to the jar:

Cheesy Popcorn Spice

1/4 cup margarine

To serve – Pop 3 cups of popcorn. Melt 1/4 cup margarine in a small pan over low heat. Stir in 1 tablespoon popcorn spice. Pour over popcorn and mix well.

# Chocolate Popcorn Spice Mix

1/2 cup confectioner's sugar
1/4 cup mini semi-sweet chocolate chips
1 tablespoon plus 2 teaspoons cocoa
1/2 teaspoon ground cinnamon
Jar – Wide mouth half-pint glass canning jar

Combine all ingredients in a small bowl; stir until well blended. Put in half-pint jar and seal.

 Attach the following recipe to the jar:

Chocolate Popcorn Spice

To serve, melt 1/4 cup margarine or butter in a saucepan over low heat. Stir in 2 tablespoons popcorn spice. Pour over 3 cups popped corn; mix well.

CHOCOLATE
POPCORN
SPICE

...te Popcorn Spice

To serve, melt 1/4 cup butter
in a small saucepan over low
heat. Stir in 2 tablespoons of
the chocolate popcorn spice.
Pour over 5 cups of popped
corn and mix well.

# Cajun Popcorn Spice Mix

4 teaspoons paprika
4 teaspoons thyme
4 teaspoons basil
4 teaspoons cumin
1 teaspoon onion powder
4 teaspoons garlic powder
2 tablespoons salt
2 teaspoons black pepper
Optional – 1 teaspoon cayenne pepper
Jar – Wide mouth half-pint glass canning jar

Combine all ingredients in a small bowl; stir until well blended.

 Attach the following recipe to the jar:

Cajun Popcorn Spice

2 tablespoons vegetable oil

To serve – Pop 3 cups of popcorn. Heat the oil in a small pan over medium heat for about a minute, then add about 1 tablespoon of the popcorn spice in the jar. Cook and stir for another minute. Pour over popcorn and mix well.

# Coffee, Tea, Cocoa

## Peach Tea Mix

1/2 cup instant tea mix
1 cup white sugar
1/2 box of peach-flavored gelatin (3 ounces)
Jar – Wide mouth pint glass canning jar

In a bowl, combine all ingredients and stir well. Put in a pint glass jar and seal.

Attach the following recipe to the jar:

Peach Tea

To make peach tea, stir 2 teaspoons of tea mix into 8 ounces hot water.

# Spiced Hot Tea Mix

1 1/4 cups Tang or other orange breakfast drink dry mix
3/4 cup iced tea mix with lemon and sugar
1/4 teaspoon ground cloves
1 teaspoon ground cinnamon
1/2 teaspoon ground allspice
Jar – Wide mouth pint glass canning jar

In a bowl, combine all the ingredients and stir well. Put in a pint glass jar and seal.

Attach the following recipe to the jar:

Spiced Hot Tea

To make spiced tea, stir 2 teaspoons of tea mix into 8 ounces hot water.

# Café Au Lait Mix

1 1/2 cups instant non-dairy creamer
1/4 cup instant coffee crystals
1/4 cup packed brown sugar
Dash salt
Jar – Wide mouth pint glass canning jar

In a bowl, combine all the ingredients and stir well. Put in a pint glass jar and seal.

Attach the following recipe to the jar:

Café Au Lait

In a cup, combine 1/4 cup of the Café Au Lait mix with 2/3 cup boiling water.

# Cinnamon Mocha Mix

2 cups sweetened cocoa mix
1/3 cup instant coffee crystals
1 teaspoon ground cinnamon
Jar – Wide mouth pint glass canning jar

In a bowl, combine all the ingredients and stir well. Put in a pint glass jar and seal.

 Attach the following recipe to the jar:

Cinnamon Mocha

In a cup, combine 2 tablespoons of the Cinnamon Mocha mix with 2/3 cup boiling water.

# Hot Chocolate Mix

2 cups instant nonfat dry milk
1/2 cup unsweetened cocoa powder
1 cup granulated sugar
1/4 teaspoon salt
Jar – Wide mouth quart glass canning jar or 2 pint canning jars

In a bowl, combine all the ingredients and stir well. Put in a quart or 2 pint glass jars and seal.

Attach the following recipe to the jar:

Hot Chocolate

Combine 1/4 cup of the hot chocolate mix with a cup of boiling water.

# Cafe Mocha Coffee Mix

3/4 cup unsweetened cocoa powder
3/4 cup granulated sugar
1/4 cup instant nonfat dry milk
Jar – Wide mouth pint glass canning jar

In a bowl, combine all the ingredients and stir well. Put in a pint glass jar and seal.

Attach the following recipe to the jar:

Cafe Mocha Coffee

Combine 2 to 3 tablespoons of the Cafe Mocha mix with a cup of hot coffee.

# Holly Jolly Coffee Mix

2/3 cup instant nonfat dry milk
2/3 cup granulated sugar
1/2 cup instant coffee
1/2 teaspoon cinnamon
Jar – Wide mouth pint glass canning jar

In a bowl, combine all the ingredients and stir well. Put in a pint glass jar and seal.

Attach the following recipe to the jar:

Holly Jolly Coffee

Combine 2 teaspoons of the Holly Jolly coffee mix with a cup of hot water.

# Jack Frost's Hot Orange Drink Mix

1 10-ounce jar of Tang or other orange breakfast drink dry mix
2 cups granulated sugar
1/4 cup of lemonade mix
2 teaspoon cinnamon
1 teaspoon cloves
Jar – Wide mouth quart glass canning jar or 2 pint jars

In a bowl, combine all the ingredients and stir well. Put in a quart or 2 pint glass jars and seal.

Attach the following recipe to the jar:

Jack Frost's Hot Orange Drink

Combine 2 1/2 teaspoons of the hot orange drink mix with a cup of boiling water.

# Fireside Coffee Mix

2/3 cup non-dairy coffee creamer
1/2 cup carnation hot cocoa mix
1/2 cup instant coffee
1/2 cup granulated sugar
1/3 teaspoon cinnamon
1/4 teaspoon nutmeg
Jar – Wide mouth pint glass canning jar

In a bowl, combine all the ingredients and stir well. Put in a pint glass jar and seal.

 Attach the following recipe to the jar:

Fireside Coffee

Combine 2 tablespoons plus 1 teaspoon of the Fireside coffee mix with a cup of boiling water.

# Hot Chocolate Mix With Marshmallows

2 cups instant nonfat dry milk
3/4 cup granulated sugar
1/2 cup unsweetened cocoa powder
1 teaspoon cinnamon
1 cup mini marshmallows
Jar – Wide mouth quart glass canning jar

Mix sugar, dry milk, cocoa and cinnamon together. Put in canning jar and pack. Add mini marshmallows on top. Seal jar.

Attach the following recipe to the jar:

Hot Chocolate Mix With Marshmallows

Combine 1/4 cup of the hot chocolate mix with a cup of boiling water.

# Soups

## Split Pea Soup Mix

2 cups dry milk powder
1 tablespoon minced onion flakes
1 teaspoon parsley flakes
1/4 teaspoon garlic powder
1/4 teaspoon salt
1/2 teaspoon pepper
1 bay leaf
16 ounces dried split peas
Jar – Wide mouth quart glass canning jar

Combine dry milk powder and all the ingredients above except the peas and bay leaf. Layer in the jar - first milk mixture, then the peas and the bay leaf on top. Seal jar.

Attach the following recipe to the jar:

Split Pea Soup

2 cups diced fully cooked ham
1 to 1 1/2 cups sliced baby carrots
7 cups boiling water

Pour the contents of the jar into a crock pot. Add boiling water. Add carrots. Cover and cook on medium high for about 5 hours. (If your crockpot dial is 1 to 5, set it at 4) Be sure to stir occasionally. Add cooked ham after 4 hours. Add more water if necessary while it cooks.

# Chicken Rice Soup Mix

3 cups uncooked long grain brown rice
3/4 cup chicken bouillon granules
2 tablespoons dried parsley
4 tablespoons dried tarragon
1 1/2 teaspoons pepper
Jar – Wide mouth quart glass canning jar

Combine all the ingredients above and put in quart jar. Seal jar.

Attach the following recipe to the jar:

Chicken Rice Soup

4 1/2 cups water
2 tablespoons margarine
Cooked chicken pieces, optional

Bring water, margarine and 1 cup of the soup mix in the jar to a boil. Reduce heat, cover and simmer for 40 minutes or until rice is tender. Add cooked chicken while simmering, if desired.

# Bean Soup Mix

*The small jewelry bags with Ziploc tops you can find at hobby stores are perfect for the spice packet created below. Or use a small plastic container for the spices.*

1 cup dried split peas
1 cup barley
1 cup dry lentils
1 cup uncooked brown or white rice
2 tablespoons parsley
1 teaspoon black pepper
2 teaspoons salt
2 tablespoons dry minced onion
2 teaspoons beef bouillon
2 teaspoons garlic powder
2 teaspoons Italian seasoning
2 teaspoons cumin
Jar – Wide mouth quart glass canning jar

Layer the first 4 ingredients in a jar. Mix all the spices together and create a spice packet in a small jewelry or Ziploc bag. Seal the jar and set the spice packet aside to attach to the outside of the jar when you attach the recipe.

 Attach the following recipe to the jar:

Bean Soup

Pour the contents of the jar into a strainer and rinse. Move contents of the strainer to a large pot and add 12 cups of water and the spice packet. Bring the soup to a boil and then lower the heat. Cover pot and simmer for 1 hour or more, stirring occasionally. More water may need to be added.

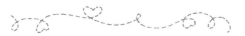

# Potato Soup Mix

*The consistency of this soup is a little thinner than most thick potato soups. But it is a great tasting soup nonetheless.*

2 1/3 cups instant mashed potato flakes
2 cups dry milk powder
3 teaspoons chicken bouillon granules
1 teaspoon onion powder
1 1/4 teaspoons dried parsley
1/4 teaspoon ground pepper
1/2 teaspoon garlic powder
1 teaspoon seasoning salt
2 tablespoons dried chives
Jar – Wide mouth quart glass canning jar

Mix all the ingredients in a bowl. Pour into the jar.

 Attach the following recipe to the jar:

Potato Soup

To serve, add one cup of boiling water to 1/2 cup of the soup mix in a bowl, and stir until smooth. Serve with chives, crumbled bacon, grated cheese and sour cream if desired.

# Chili

## Cold Weather Chili Mix

1 teaspoon salt
1/4 teaspoon oregano
1 teaspoon chili powder
1/4 teaspoon paprika
1/2 teaspoon garlic salt
1 tablespoon dried onion
Jar –one half-pint jar

Mix all the spices together in the half-pint jar.

 Attach the following recipe to the jar:

Cold Weather Chili

1 lb. lean hamburger
1 (15 oz.) can of pinto beans or ranch-style beans
1 quart tomatoes
1 can (10.75 oz.) tomato soup

Brown hamburger and drain. Add all the rest of the ingredients plus the contents of the jar. Simmer about 1 hour.

## Easy Vegetarian Chili Mix

*By putting the chili spices in individual containers, the recipient can add as much or as little of a spice as they want. Also add the cans of beans, tomatoes and veggie flavor packets so they will have everything they need to make the chili. Use little pieces of tin foil to mix the spices, then bend the foil into little funnels and fill the small jars. Labels are available online for the cans.*

2 packets Swanson vegetable flavor boost
6 oz. can of tomato paste
2 cans ranch style beans
1 (28 oz.) can petit diced tomatoes

*Little jar one:*
1/4 teaspoon red pepper
1 tablespoon chili powder

*Little jar two:*
1/3 teaspoon cumin
1 teaspoon oregano
1/2 teaspoon garlic powder
1/2 teaspoon salt

*Little jar three:*
1 tablespoon dried onion

*Little jar four:*
3 tablespoons masa flour

Jars – small glass jars (from a hobby store) or small plastic containers

Attach the following recipe to the jar:

Easy Vegetarian Chili

In a pot, combine vegetable packets and 1 cup of water. Drain and rinse beans. Add all the rest of the ingredients to the pot, cover and cook on low for 4 to 6 hours. This chili can also be cooked in a crock pot.

# Quick and Spicy Chili Mix

1 teaspoon dried onion flakes
1 teaspoon garlic powder
1 1/2 teaspoons red pepper
2 tablespoons chili powder
3/4 teaspoon salt
1/2 teaspoon black pepper
Jars – several very small jars or one half-pint jar

If using a half-pint jar, mix all the spices together. Otherwise combine spices to fit in the smaller jars you are using.

Attach the following recipe to the jar:

Quick and Spicy Chili

1 lb. lean hamburger
Small can of corn, 8 oz.
1 can pinto beans, 15 oz.
Can of tomato paste, 6 oz.
Can of tomato sauce, 8 oz.
1 jalapeno pepper, chopped (optional)

Brown hamburger and drain. In a large pot, mix corn, beans, tomato paste, tomato sauce and one cup of water. Add the contents of the jar. Bring to a boil and then reduce heat to medium-low. Mix in cooked hamburger. Cook 45 minutes to 1 hour, stirring occasionally.

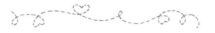

# Nuts & Snacks

## Hollandaise Snack Mix

1 cup unsalted dry-roasted peanuts
1 cup Ritz bits crackers
1 cup stick pretzels
1/2 cup butter
1 teaspoon garlic powder
1 package hollandaise sauce mix, .9 ounces
1 tablespoon Worcestershire sauce
Jar – Wide mouth quart glass canning jar

Preheat oven to 300 degrees F. In a small saucepan, melt butter over medium heat. Stir in garlic powder, hollandaise sauce and Worcestershire sauce. In a large bowl, mix together crackers, peanuts and pretzels. Pour butter mixture over the dry mixture. Toss until well coated.

Spread evenly on a baking sheet. Bake 15 to 20 minutes, stirring occasionally. Remove from baking sheet to cool. Spread on waxed paper or foil to cool, about 15 minutes. When completely cool, pack in quart jar and seal.

# Ranch Oyster Crackers

*It takes 2 cups of these to fill a pint glass canning jar, 4 cups to fill a quart glass canning jar. This recipe makes 6 cups so it will fill 3 pint jars or 1 quart and 1 pint jars.*

1 package oyster crackers (12 oz.)
1/2 cup vegetable oil
1/2 teaspoon dried dill weed
1 envelope Ranch dry salad dressing mix
Jar – Wide mouth pint or quart glass canning jar

Preheat oven to 200 degrees F. In a large bowl, combine Ranch salad dressing mix, oil and dill weed. Mix well and add crackers. Toss until well coated. Spread the seasoned oyster crackers on a cookie sheet and bake for 15 to 20 minutes, stirring once halfway through. Let cool before packing in jars.

*Tip: Line cookie sheet with parchment paper before baking and you can just slide the paper off onto the counter to let the crackers cool.*

# Granola

*This recipe will fill about 3 quart jars.*

1 cup brown sugar packed
1/2 cup water
4 teaspoon vanilla
8 cups uncooked old fashioned oatmeal
2 cups pecans and almonds
2 cups any dried fruit
Jars – 3 wide mouth quart glass canning jars

Preheat oven to 275 degrees F. Mix sugar and water together. Place in microwave safe bowl and microwave on medium high for 5 minutes. Add vanilla. Place oats and nuts in large bowl. Pour syrup mixture over oats and nuts and mix well.

Place mixture on 2 ungreased jelly roll pans. Bake for 45 to 60 minutes; stirring and tuning every 15 minutes. Cool and then add dried fruit. Fill quart jars when cooled and seal.

# Hurricane Snacks

*Just using the red and green M&M's at Christmas will make this snack jar look festive. Use the all-colored M&M's for a colorful jar the rest of year. A bag of just red M&M's and just green M&M's can be purchased online if you can't find the holiday colors anywhere else. This recipe is easy enough for the kids to make for gifts.*

1 cup dry roasted peanuts
1 1/4 cups M&M's
1 cup chocolate covered peanuts
1 (5 ounce) bag of Craisins
Jar – Wide mouth quart glass canning jar or 2 pint canning jars

This snack can be packed one of two ways – the first, just mix roasted and chocolate peanuts, M&M's and Craisins together in a large bowl and fill a quart jar. The second, layer each ingredient in a jar without mixing anything.

# Reindeer Chow

1 1/2 cup semi-sweet chocolate chips
1/2 cup peanut butter
1 (15 oz.) box Rice Chex or Crispix
1 1/2 cup confectioners' sugar
1/4 cup margarine
Jar – Wide mouth quart glass canning

Melt chocolate chips, peanut butter, and margarine together. Pour Rice Chex into a very large bowl. When chocolate mixture has melted, pour over Rice Chex, stirring gently to coat. Add confectioners' sugar. Cover bowl, shake gently to coat. Pour out in single layer to dry and put in quart jar when cool.

# Snack Scrabble

6 teaspoons margarine
1/2 teaspoon onion salt
1/2 teaspoon seasoned salt or garlic salt
4 teaspoons Worcestershire sauce
4 cups Chex cereal any combination, wheat, corn or rice
1 small package pretzels
1 can mixed nuts
Jar – Wide mouth quart glass canning jar

Preheat oven to 250 degrees F. Melt margarine and add the salts and Worcestershire sauce. Put cereal, nuts and pretzels into a 9 x 13 pan. Pour sauce over cereal and mix until coated. Bake for 45 minutes stirring every 15 minutes. Drain on paper towels.

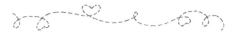

# Mixed Spiced Nuts

1 egg white, slightly beaten
2/3 cup whole almonds
2 cups dry roasted peanuts
3/4 cup granulated sugar
2/3 cup walnut halves
3/4 teaspoon salt
1 teaspoon of pumpkin pie spice
1 teaspoon of water
Jar – Wide mouth quart glass canning jar

Preheat oven to 300 degrees F. Combine egg white and water together. Add nuts and toss to coat. Combine pumpkin pie spice, sugar and salt. Add this to the nuts and toss until the nuts are coated.

Spread evenly on a greased baking sheet. Bake for 20 to 25 minutes. Cool nuts on waxed paper. Break up any large clusters. Pour out in single layer to cool on wax paper and put in jar when cool.

# Spicy Chili Peanuts

*These will fill 2 pint canning jars.*

36 ounces of cocktail peanuts (or 4 cups)
1 package chili seasoning mix (1 5/8 ounces)
1/2 cup margarine, melted
Jars – 2 wide mouth pint glass canning jars

Put peanuts in a crockpot. Pour melted margarine over nuts, then sprinkle with the chili mix. Toss until well mixed. Cover and cook on low for 2 to 2 1/2 hours. Remove crockpot lid and cook nuts on high for 10 to 15 minutes. Pour out in single layer to cool on wax paper and put in jar when cool.

# Holiday Candied Pecans

4 cups pecan halves
1 cup granulated sugar
1 tablespoon cinnamon
1 teaspoon salt
1 egg white
2 tablespoons water
Jar – Wide mouth quart glass canning jar or 2 pint jars

Preheat oven to 250 degrees F. Mix water and egg white together in a bowl. Mix salt, sugar and cinnamon together in another bowl.

Dip pecans in the egg white mixture with a slotted cooking spoon, then dip the pecans into the dry mixture and shake off excess. Place them on a cookie sheet lined with parchment paper and bake for 1 hour, stirring them every 15 minutes. Cool and pack in jars.

# Santa's Spiced Walnuts

4 cups of walnuts
1 cup granulated sugar
1/4 teaspoon nutmeg
1/4 teaspoon ginger
1 teaspoon cinnamon
1/4 cup water
Jar – Wide mouth quart glass canning jar or 2 pint jars

Add water, spices and sugar to a large skillet. Bring to a boil and cook until  mixture thickens. Remove from heat. Add walnuts to the pan and coat with mixture. Spread nuts out on wax paper, separate them and let them cool. After nuts are cool, pack in jars and seal.

# Spicy Football Snack

2/3 cup Wheat Chex
2/3 cup Corn Chex
2/3 cup Cheerios
2/3 cup Cheez-It
2/3 cup pretzels
2/3 cup mixed nuts
1/3 cup margarine
3/4 teaspoon garlic powder
1 tablespoon Worcestershire sauce
Jar – Wide mouth quart glass canning jar

Preheat oven to 225 degrees F. Combine the first 6 ingredients in a large bowl and set aside.

Melt margarine in microwave. Add garlic powder and Worcestershire sauce to  margarine and stir until well blended. Pour over the dry mixture and stir until dry mixture is evenly coated.

Spread cereal mixture on a cookie sheet. Bake for 1 hour, stirring occasionally. Cool on wax paper or parchment paper. Pack in jar when cool.

# Spicy Almonds

1 egg white
4 teaspoons granulated sugar
3 teaspoons garlic salt
1 1/2 teaspoons black pepper
1/2 teaspoon red pepper
2 teaspoons ground cumin
1 teaspoon chili powder
3 1/2 cups whole almonds with the skins on
Jar – Wide mouth quart glass canning jar or 2 pint jars

Preheat oven to 275 degrees F. Beat 1 egg white in large bowl until frothy. Add sugar, garlic salt, red pepper, black pepper, cumin, chili powder and almonds with skins. Stir to coat almonds evenly and place almonds in single layer on a greased cookie sheet.

Bake for 40 minutes, stirring every 10 minutes. Remove from oven and cool. When cool, pack in jars.

# Ranch Snack Mix

1 cup miniature pretzels
1 cup Bugles or Chex
1 cup salted cashews
1 cup bite-size cheddar cheese fish crackers
1/2 cup vegetable oil
1 envelope ranch salad dressing mix
Jar – Wide mouth quart glass canning jar

Combine pretzels, cashews, Bugles and crackers in a large bowl. Sprinkle with salad dressing mix and toss to mix. Drizzle with oil and mix until well coated. Spread on waxed paper or foil to dry before packing in jars.

# Super Spicy Pecans

4 cups pecan halves
3 tablespoons margarine
3 tablespoons Worcestershire sauce
1/4 teaspoon garlic powder
1 teaspoon salt
1/2 teaspoon cinnamon
1/4 teaspoon cayenne pepper
Dash of bottled pepper sauce
Jar – Wide mouth quart glass canning jar

Preheat oven to 300 degrees F. In a heavy skillet, melt margarine. Stir in the rest of the ingredients except nuts and mix well.

Add pecans and stir until nuts are coated well. Bake for 20 - 25 minutes until nuts turn crispy and brown, stirring often. Let cool before packing in jar.

# Dried Fruit

Use 26 ounces of dried fruit, such as dried banana chips, apricots, cranberries, pineapple, papaya and raisins.

The packages of dried fruit that weigh between 5 ounces and 7 ounces are perfect.

Jar – Wide mouth quart glass canning jar

Layer the dried fruit in a canning jar. 5 or 6 different types of dried fruit is sufficient and the colorful the better. Seal the jar.

# White Chocolate Pretzel Mix

1 1/4 cups crisp rice cereal
1 1/4 cups salted peanuts
1 1/4 cups pretzel sticks
10 1-ounce squares white baking chocolate
2 teaspoons margarine
Jar – Wide mouth quart glass canning jar

Combine cereal, peanuts and pretzels in a large bowl. Melt chocolate and margarine in a microwave, stirring until melted. Pour over dry mixture and mix to coat evenly. Drop by heaping spoonfuls on waxed paper. Let cool before packing in jars.

# Trail Mix

2 2/3 cups Honey-Nut Cheerios
3/4 cup peanuts
1/3 cup dried cranberries
1/3 cup carob chips
1/4 cup sunflower seeds
Jar – Wide mouth quart glass canning jar

Mix all ingredients together in a large bowl and fill a quart jar. Seal the jar.

# Honey Cranberry Snack Mix

*This recipe fills 2 quart jars or 4 pints and makes up very quickly.*

1/4 cup Creamy Peanut Butter & Honey
1/4 cup butter
1/2 teaspoon vanilla
1 teaspoon ground cinnamon
4 cups Honey Nut Chex
1 cup mini pretzels
1 cup honey roasted peanuts
1 cup dried cranberries
Jar – 2 wide mouth quart glass canning jar

Heat oven to 350 degrees F. Mix peanuts, cereal, cranberries and pretzels in a large bowl. In a small bowl, combine cinnamon and vanilla. Combine butter and peanut butter in a microwave-safe bowl. Microwave on high for 25 seconds. Remove from microwave and add cinnamon and vanilla. Stir quickly until well blended. Microwave for another 10 seconds. Pour half the hot mixture over the dry cereal mixture, stir, then add the other half of the hot mixture and stir until well coated.

Line a cookie sheet with foil. Spread the mixture evenly on cookie sheet. Bake for 5 minutes, stir and bake for another 5 minutes. Transfer mixture to a clean piece of tin foil to cool.

# Almond Bark Snack Mix

*This recipe makes enough to fill 3 quart jars. This mix should be left loose in the jars, rather than packed. I took these snacks to work and they are still asking for more.*

2 cups chocolate Chex cereal
1 cup Honey Nut Cheerios
1 cup mini pretzels
1 cup pecan halves
1 cup honey roasted peanuts
1 cup M&M's
1 package almond bark (12 ounces)
Jar – 3 wide mouth quart glass canning jars

In a large bowl, combine pretzels, nuts and cereal. In a bowl, microwave  almond bark at 50% power for 1 minute. Stir and microwave for 1 more minute at 50% power. Stir almond bark until mixed and pour over the cereal mixture, stirring until coated evenly.

Spread on wax paper or parchment paper until cool. Break into pieces. Let cool before packing in jars. Either add M&M's before filling jars, or layer half the snack mix, then M&M's, then the rest of the snack mix.

Almond Bark Snack layers *not* mixed in jar

Almond Bark Snack layers mixed in jar

# Muffins

## Muffin Brownie Mix

1 cup all-purpose flour
1 3/4 cups granulated sugar
1 1/4 cup chopped pecans
3/4 cups semi-sweet chocolate chips
Jar – Wide mouth quart glass canning jar

Layer flour, chips, sugar and pecans in a jar, packing the flour and sugar layers, ending with the chocolate chips. Be sure to put chocolate chips on top. Seal jar.

Attach the following recipe to the jar:

Muffin Brownies

1 cup margarine, melted
4 slightly beaten eggs
1 teaspoon vanilla

Preheat oven to 325 degrees F. Carefully remove just the chocolate chips from the jar. Melt chocolate chips and margarine over medium heat or microwave. Cool. Stir in vanilla, eggs and remaining contents of the jar. Spoon batter into greased or paper-lined muffin tins. Bake about 30 minutes or until toothpick inserted in center comes out clean.

# Spiced Applesauce Muffin Mix

1 1/2 cups all-purpose flour
1 teaspoon cinnamon
1 teaspoon allspice
2 teaspoons baking powder
1/2 teaspoon baking soda
2/3 cup brown sugar
1/2 cup raisins
Jar – Wide mouth pint glass canning jar

Mix flour, spices, baking powder and soda together. Layer flour mixture, sugar then raisins in the jar. Seal jar.

Attach the following recipe to the jar:

Spiced Applesauce Muffins

1/2 cup margarine
2 eggs
1 cup applesauce
1/4 teaspoon vanilla

Preheat oven to 350 degrees F. In a large bowl, mix together margarine, vanilla and eggs and beat until smooth. Mix in the contents of the jar. Stir until well blended. Mix in applesauce. Line a muffin pan with paper liners. Pour batter into muffin cups and fill about 2/3 full. Bake for 20 to 25 minutes until toothpick inserted comes out clean.

# Double Chocolate Muffin Mix

1 2/3 cups all-purpose flour
1/2 teaspoon baking soda
1/4 teaspoon salt
1 3/4 teaspoons baking powder
1/3 cup cocoa powder
1 1/4 cups granulated sugar
3/4 cup chocolate chips
1/2 cup chopped walnuts
Jar – Wide mouth quart glass canning jar

Mix flour, baking soda, baking powder and salt together. Layer flour mixture, cocoa powder, granulated sugar, chocolate chips and walnuts in the jar. Seal jar.

 Attach the following recipe to the jar:

Double Chocolate Muffins

1 cup milk
1 egg
2 tablespoons vegetable oil
3/4 teaspoon vanilla

Preheat oven to 350 degrees F. In a large bowl, mix together milk, egg, vanilla and oil. Add contents of the jar and mix well. Line muffin cups with paper muffin liners or grease muffin cups. Fill muffin cups 3/4 full. Bake for 20 to 25 minutes or until toothpick inserted comes out clean.

# Blueberry Muffin Mix

2 cups all-purpose flour
1/2 teaspoon salt
2 teaspoons baking powder
1 1/4 cups granulated sugar
1 cup dried blueberries
Jar – Wide mouth quart glass canning jar

In a large bowl, stir together flour, baking powder and salt. Layer flour mixture in a jar and pack. Add granulated sugar next, then blueberries. Seal jar.

Attach the following recipe to the jar:

Blueberry Muffins

1/2 cup butter
2 eggs
1/4 cup milk
Topping: 1/4 cup granulated sugar

Preheat oven to 375 degrees F. Lightly grease a muffin pan or use paper liners. Mix butter, milk and eggs in a large bowl. Add all the ingredients from the jar.

Fill muffin cups 3/4 full and sprinkle with the (topping) 1/4 cup of sugar. Bake for 30 minutes.

# Apple Spice Muffin Mix

*With this jar recipe, be sure to put the dried apples on the very top. Since they don't pack, anything you put on top of them (like sugar) will just fall down into the apples and the apples actually disappear from the outside of the jar.*

2 cups all-purpose flour
2 teaspoons baking powder
1 teaspoon allspice
1 teaspoon cinnamon
1/2 teaspoon salt
1/2 cup granulated sugar
1/4 cup brown sugar
1 cup chopped dried apples
Jar – Wide mouth quart glass canning jar

Mix flour, baking powder, allspice, cinnamon and salt together. Layer flour mixture, brown sugar, granulated sugar and apples in the jar. Seal jar. *(Note: The brown sugar can be built up on the front of the jar for display since there isn't much brown sugar.)*

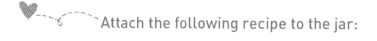 Attach the following recipe to the jar:

Apple Spice Muffins

1 egg, beaten
1/4 cup vegetable oil
3/4 cup milk

Preheat oven to 400 degrees F. Mix together egg, milk and vegetable oil. Add  contents of the jar into the bowl and mix well. Grease muffin cups or use paper muffin liners and fill about 3/4 full. Bake 15 to18 minutes or until golden brown.

Apple Spice Muffins

# Chocolate Chip Muffin Mix

2 3/4 cups all-purpose flour
1 tablespoon and 1 teaspoon baking powder
3/4 teaspoon salt
2/3 cup granulated sugar
1 cup semi-sweet chocolate chips
Jar – Wide mouth quart glass canning jar

Combine flour, salt and baking powder. Layer in jar in this order: flour mixture, sugar then chocolate chips in jar. Seal jar.

 Attach the following recipe to the jar:

Chocolate Chip Muffins

1 cup milk
1 egg
1/3 cup vegetable oil
Topping: 3 tablespoons granulated sugar, 3 tablespoons brown sugar

Preheat oven to 400 degrees F. Mix oil, egg and milk in a large bowl. Add contents of jar and stir well. Lightly grease muffin tins or line with baking cups. Fill muffin cups 2/3 full. Mix granulated sugar and brown sugar (topping) together and sprinkle on top of the muffins before baking. Bake for 20 to 25 minutes or until toothpick inserted comes out clean.

# Harvest Muffin Mix

1 1/2 cups all-purpose flour
1/4 teaspoon nutmeg
1 teaspoon cinnamon
1 1/2 teaspoon baking powder
1/4 teaspoon salt
1/4 teaspoon baking soda
1/2 teaspoon ginger
1/4 cup and 2 tablespoons brown sugar
1/4 cup and 2 tablespoons granulated sugar
1/2 cup dried cranberries, chopped
1/2 cup dried apple, chopped
1/4 cup toasted hazelnuts, chopped
1/4 cup dried figs, chopped
Jar – Wide mouth quart glass canning jar

In a large bowl, stir together flour, baking soda, baking powder, salt, cinnamon, nutmeg and ginger. Layer flour mixture first in a jar and pack. Add brown sugar and granulated sugar. Add the fruit and nuts in layers on top. Seal jar.

Attach the following recipe to the jar:

Harvest Muffins

1/2 cup butter, melted
1 egg, beaten
1/2 cup and 2 tablespoons milk

Preheat oven to 375 degrees F. Grease muffin pans or line with paper muffin liners.

In a large bowl, add the contents of the jar. Make a well in the center and add melted butter, milk and egg. Mix until smooth. Spoon batter into the muffin pans to 3/4 full. Bake for 15 to 20 minutes or until a toothpick inserted comes out clean.

# Oatmeal Muffin Mix

*Pack these ingredients firmly in a jar and they will all fit in a pint canning jar.*

1 cup all-purpose flour
1/2 teaspoon baking soda
1 teaspoon baking powder
Pinch of salt
3/4 cup Quaker oats (oatmeal)
2/3 cup brown sugar
Jar – Wide mouth pint glass canning jar

Mix flour, baking soda, salt and baking powder. Layer flour mixture in the jar, followed by brown sugar and oats. Seal jar.

 Attach the following recipe to the jar:

Oatmeal Muffins

2 eggs
1/2 cup milk
1/2 cup vegetable oil

Preheat oven to 400 degrees F. Mix eggs, milk and vegetable oil together. Add contents of the jar and mix well. Fill muffin cups 2/3 full (use muffin liners or spray cups with vegetable oil spray). Bake for 20 minutes or until inserted toothpick comes out clean.

# Bars

## Scratch Brownie Mix

1 1/8 cups all-purpose flour
3/4 teaspoon salt
3/4 cup cocoa powder
2 1/4 cups granulated sugar
3/4 cup semi-sweet chocolate chips
Jar – Wide mouth quart glass canning jar

Mix together the flour and salt. Layer in jar with the flour mixture first, then cocoa powder, sugar and chocolate chips on top in case everything doesn't fit. Pack the layers well and it should all fit in the jar.

Attach the following recipe to the jar:

Scratch Brownies

3/4 cup margarine or butter, melted
3 eggs, beaten
2 1/4 teaspoons vanilla

Preheat oven to 350 degrees F. Empty contents of the jar into a large bowl. Make a well in the center of the dry ingredients and add margarine, vanilla and eggs. Mix well. Spread batter into a greased 9" x 13" baking pan. Bake for 35 to 40 minutes. Cool in pan.

# Apple Bars Mix

1 cup all-purpose flour
3/4 teaspoon cinnamon
1/2 teaspoon baking soda
1/2 teaspoon salt
1/2 cup brown sugar
1 cup oatmeal
1 3/4 cups dried apples
1/2 cup walnuts, chopped
Jar – Wide mouth quart glass canning jar

Mix flour, baking soda, salt and cinnamon together. In the jar, layer flour mixture, brown sugar, oatmeal, walnuts and apples on top, packing each layer. Be sure apples and walnuts are on top, because in the instructions below, they will be removed from the jar and set aside. Seal the jar.

Attach the following recipe to the jar:

Apple Bars

1/2 cup shortening (Crisco)
2 tablespoons margarine
1/4 cup granulated sugar

Preheat oven to 350 degrees F. Grease bottom of an 8 or 9-inch baking pan. Remove the apples and walnuts from the jar and set aside. Empty the contents of the jar in a large bowl. Cut in shortening until mixture is of a crumbly texture. Evenly spread half of this crumble mixture in the bottom of greased pan. Dot surface with margarine and then spread the apples in pan. Mix 1/4 cup sugar and walnuts. Sprinkle walnuts and sugar mixture on top. Finish by topping it off with the remaining half of the crumble mixture. Bake for 40 to 45 minutes.

# Raisin Carrot Bar Mix

1 package carrot cake mix
3/4 cup raisins
1/2 cup chopped walnuts
Jar – Wide mouth quart glass canning jar

Layer the ingredients above in a jar in this order – carrot cake mix, raisins, then nuts and seal jar.

Attach the following recipe to the jar:

Raisin Carrot Bars

1/2 cup vegetable oil
1/4 cup water
2 eggs
1 can of cream cheese frosting

Preheat oven to 350°. Mix contents of the jar, water, vegetable oil and eggs in a large bowl. Spread evenly in pan. Grease and flour a jelly roll pan, 15×10×1 inch. Bake 15 to 20 minutes or until bars spring back when touched lightly in center. Cool then frost with can of frosting. Cut into bars.

# Chocolate Chip Squares Mix

1 cup packed brown sugar
2 cups all-purpose flour
1 cup semi-sweet chocolate chips
Jar – Wide mouth quart glass canning jar

In the jar, layer flour, brown sugar and chocolate chips, packing each layer except the chocolate chips. Seal the jar.

Attach the following recipe to the jar:

Chocolate Chip Squares

1 cup butter, melted
1 teaspoon vanilla extract

Preheat oven to 350 degrees F. In a large bowl, mix together melted butter or margarine and vanilla. Add contents of the jar and mix well. Press in an ungreased jelly roll pan or cookie sheet. Bake for 20 minutes.

## Frosted Coffee Bar Mix

3 cups all-purpose flour
1/4 teaspoon salt
1 teaspoon baking powder
1 teaspoon baking soda
1 teaspoon cinnamon
2 cups brown sugar
1 cup raisins
1/2 cup nuts
Jar – Wide mouth quart glass canning jar

Mix flour, baking soda, baking powder, salt and cinnamon together. In the jar, layer flour mixture, brown sugar, raisins and nuts. Seal the jar.

 Attach the following recipe to the jar:

Frosted Coffee Bars

1/2 cup margarine or butter
1 cup coffee
2 eggs
1 teaspoon vanilla
Confectioners' sugar for top

Preheat oven to 350 degrees F. In a large bowl, mix butter and eggs together, then add vanilla and coffee. Add contents of the jar and mix well. Bake in 9" x 13" greased cake pan for 15 to 20 minutes.

*Optional Confectioners' Sugar Frosting*

1 1/2 cups confectioners' sugar
3 tablespoons butter, softened
1 tablespoon milk
1 tablespoon vanilla

Combine all the above, beating until creamy. Frost the coffee bars with a thin layer while they are still warm. Add a little more milk to thin the consistency if needed. Note: For coffee flavor in the frosting, add 1/2 teaspoon instant coffee granules and 1 1/2 tablespoons cocoa powder to frosting.

# Butterscotch Square Mix

1 1/2 cup all-purpose flour
2 teaspoons baking powder
1 cup brown sugar
1 cup granulated sugar
3/4 cup pecans or walnuts
Jar – Wide mouth quart glass canning jar

Mix flour and baking powder, then layer the flour mixture, sugars and nuts on top, being sure to pack each layer. Be sure to pack the nuts on top so they can be removed from the jar and set aside when baking.

Attach the following recipe to the jar:

Butterscotch Squares

1 cup butter, melted
2 eggs beaten
2 teaspoons vanilla

Preheat oven to 350 degrees F. Remove nuts from the jar and set aside. Mix eggs, butter and vanilla. Add the rest of the contents of the jar. Cover the bottom of a 9" x 13" greased pan with nuts. Pour mixture over nuts and bake for 20 to 30 minutes.

# Coconut Chocolate Bar Mix

1 2/3 cups crushed graham crackers
1 2/3 cups shredded coconut
1/2 cup chocolate chips
Jar – Wide mouth quart glass canning jar

Layer each ingredient above in a jar and seal.

Attach the following recipe to the jar:

Coconut Chocolate Bars

1 3/4 cups sweet condensed milk

Preheat oven to 350 degrees F. Pour the contents of the jar into a large bowl. Mix well, and then add condensed milk. Stir until well blended. Grease a 9" baking pan. Press mixture evenly into baking pan. Bake for 30 minutes.

# Energy Bar Mix

1/2 teaspoon cinnamon
3/4 cup whole wheat flour
1/2 teaspoon salt
1 2/3 cups rolled oats
1/3 brown sugar, packed
1/4 cup flax seeds
1/3 cup wheat germ
1/4 sunflower seeds
1/4 sesame seeds
1/4 semi-sweet chocolate chips
Jar – Wide mouth quart glass canning jar

Mix flour, salt and cinnamon together. Place flour mixture in jar and then layer the rest of the ingredients. Seal the jar.

Attach the following recipe to the jar:

Energy Bars

1 egg, beaten
1/3 cup honey
1/3 cup canola oil
3/4 teaspoon vanilla

Preheat oven to 350 degrees F. Mix egg, honey, canola oil and vanilla together in a large bowl. Add the mixture from the jar and stir until well mixed. Press  mixture into a 9" x 13" lightly greased pan. Bake for 20 to 25 minutes or until edges are lightly browned.

# Blonde Brownie Mix

2 cups all-purpose flour
1 1/2 tablespoons baking powder
1/4 teaspoon salt
2/3 cup chopped pecans
1/2 cup coconut
2 cups packed brown sugar

Mix flour, baking powder and salt together. Layer ingredients in the order above in the jar. Press each layer firmly in place.

 Attach the following recipe to the jar:

Blonde Brownies

3/4 cup margarine
2 eggs, beaten slightly
2 teaspoons vanilla

Preheat oven to 375 degrees F. Pour the jar mixture into a large bowl and stir until mixed. Add margarine, eggs and vanilla. Mix until blended. Spread batter in a lightly greased 13 x 9 inch pan. Bake for 25 minutes. Cut into bars. Makes 2 dozen brownies.

# Granola Coconut Bar Mix

2 cups old-fashioned oats
2/3 cup semi-sweet chocolate chips
1/2 cup packed brown sugar
1/3 cup flaked coconut
1/3 cup walnuts
1/3 cup raisins
Jar – Wide mouth quart glass canning jar

In the jar, layer all the ingredients as listed above. Seal the jar.

Attach the following recipe to the jar:

Granola Coconut Bars

1/2 cup peanut butter
1 1/2 teaspoons vanilla
1/3 cup honey or corn syrup
1/3 cup margarine, melted

Preheat oven to 325 degrees F. In a large bowl, combine corn syrup, peanut butter, margarine and vanilla. Add jar of mix and stir until mixed well. Press into a greased 13 x 9 inch glass baking pan. Bake for 20 to 25 minutes. Cut into bars.

# Raisin Peanut Bar Mix

1/4 cup firmly packed light-brown sugar
2 cups Spoon Size Shredded Wheat, crushed
3/4 cup seedless raisins
Jar – Wide mouth quart glass canning jar

Layer brown sugar first in a jar, pack firmly, and then add raisins. Add shredded wheat last. The brown sugar needs to be the first packed layer so it can be separated for the recipe below.

Attach the following recipe to the jar:

Raisin Peanut Bars

1/4 cup corn syrup
1/4 cup chunky peanut butter

Empty contents of the jar in a bowl, except the bottom brown sugar layer. The brown sugar is packed in the jar and should remain in the jar if the other ingredients are just poured out.

Combine brown sugar (bottom layer of jar) and corn syrup in a pan. Over medium-high heat, stir until sugar dissolves. Remove pan from heat and mix in peanut butter. Stir in rest of ingredients from the jar until well coated. Press into lightly greased 8"x8" baking pan.

# Holiday Bar Mix

3 cups Rice Krispies
1/2 cup chocolate chips
1/2 cup butterscotch chips
Jar – Wide mouth quart glass canning jar

In the jar, layer chips, then cereal. Be sure to put the cereal on top so they can dump the cereal out separately. Seal the jar.

Attach the following recipe to the jar:

Holiday Bars

3/4 cups peanut butter
1/2 cup light corn syrup
1/2 cup granulated sugar

Grease bottom of a 9x13-inch cake pan. Combine peanut butter, corn syrup and sugar in a large saucepan and stir over low heat until smooth. Be sure to stir constantly to avoid burning the mixture.

Pour just the cereal from the jar into a large bowl. Pour syrup mixture over cereal and mix through. Pat into cake pan and sprinkle surface with chocolate and butterscotch chips. Warm bars in the oven or microwave until chips have melted enough to spread easily over bars. Allow bars to cool then cut into squares for serving.

# Chocolaty Bar Mix

2 cups all-purpose flour
1/4 teaspoon salt
1 cup brown sugar (packed)
1 cup chocolate chips
Jar - 1 wide mouth quart canning jar

Mix flour and salt together. Layer flour mixture, brown sugar then chocolate chips in the jar. Be sure chocolate chips are the last layer so they can be removed and set aside in the recipe below.

 Attach the following recipe to the jar:

Chocolaty Bars

1 cup butter softened
1 egg yolk
1 teaspoon vanilla

Remove chocolate chips from the jar and set aside.

Heat oven to 350 degrees F. Grease a 9" x 13" baking pan. Mix butter, egg yolk and vanilla thoroughly. Blend in brown sugar and flour mixture from the jar. Press evenly in bottom of pan. Bake 25 to 30 minutes until light brown. Remove from oven and immediately place the chocolate chips on top. When chocolate has softened, spread evenly over the top.

# Date Nut Bar Mix

3/4 cup all-purpose flour
1 cup granulated sugar
1 cup pecans, chopped
1 cup dates, chopped
Jar – Wide mouth quart glass canning jar

Layer in jar in this order: flour, sugar, pecans, then dates. Seal jar.

Attach the following recipe to the jar:

Date Nut Bars

1/2 cup vegetable oil
1 teaspoon vanilla
2 eggs
Confectioners' sugar, (optional)

Preheat oven to 350 degrees F. Mix oil, vanilla and eggs together with the ingredients from the jar. Pour into a 9 x 13" baking pan. Bake for 20 minutes. Sprinkle with confectioners' sugar after cutting.

## Fruit Bar Mix

3/4 cup all-purpose flour
1/2 teaspoon baking soda
1/2 teaspoon nutmeg
1/2 teaspoon cinnamon
1/2 teaspoon ground cloves
1/2 teaspoon salt
1 cup chopped nuts
1 cup chopped raisins
Jar – Wide mouth quart glass canning jar

Combine flour, baking soda, nutmeg, cinnamon, cloves and salt. Layer in jar in this order: flour mixture, nuts and then raisins. Seal jar.

Attach the following recipe to the jar:

Fruit Bars

1/2 cup margarine, melted
1/2 cup molasses
2 eggs, well beaten

Preheat oven to 375 degrees F. Combine margarine, molasses and eggs in a large bowl. Add fruit bar mix from the jar and stir until well blended. Pour into a greased 9" x 9" baking pan. Bake for 25 to 30 minutes. Cool and cut into squares.

# North Pole S'mores Mix

*When the weather outside is too cold for campfire s'mores, here's the next best thing. This gooey sweet dessert is a great hit with kids and Santa's helpers.*

2 cups graham cracker crumbs
1 1/2 cups miniature marshmallows
1 cup semi-sweet chocolate chips
1/8 cup granulated sugar
Jar – Wide mouth quart glass canning jar

Layer all the above ingredients in a jar in this order: sugar, graham cracker crumbs, chocolate chips, mini marshmallows. Be sure chocolate chips and marshmallows are the last layers so they can be removed and set aside in the recipe below. Seal jar.

Attach the following recipe to the jar:

North Pole S'mores

1/2 cup margarine, melted

Preheat oven to 350 degrees F. Spray cooking spray in a 9 inch square baking dish. Remove mini marshmallows and chocolate chips from the jar; set aside.

Pour the rest of the contents of jar in a large bowl and add melted margarine. Stir until well mixed. Press half of this crumb mixture in the bottom of the baking dish and bake for

5 minutes. Layer chocolate chips, then marshmallows on top of graham cracker mixture. Press remaining crumb mixture on top. Bake for 10 minutes, until marshmallows are melted. Cool and cut into bars.

# Chocolate Oatmeal Bar Mix

3/4 cup brown sugar
2 cups quick cooking oats
1 1/2 cups chocolate chips
1/2 cup walnut pieces or slivered almonds
Jar – Wide mouth quart glass canning jar

Layer brown sugar and oatmeal in the jar and pack. On top, layer chocolate chips and walnuts, and seal. Be sure to put the chocolate chips and walnuts on top so they can be removed easily and set aside when baking.

Attach the following recipe to the jar:

Chocolate Oatmeal Bars

1/2 cup butter, melted
1 teaspoon vanilla

Preheat oven to 350 degrees F. Remove nuts and chocolate chips from the jar and set aside. Combine melted butter and vanilla in a large bowl, and then add the rest of the ingredients from the jar. Bake in 8" x 8" pan at 350 degrees F for 20 minutes. Immediately sprinkle chocolate chips on top. Let stand 5 minutes or until melted. Spread the chocolate over the bars and sprinkle with nuts.

# Cinnamon Coffee Cake Mix

3/4 cup granulated sugar
1 cup all-purpose flour
1 1/2 teaspoon baking powder
1/4 teaspoon salt
Jar – Wide mouth pint glass canning jar

Mix flour, baking powder, sugar and salt together. Place flour mixture in jar and seal the jar.

Attach the following recipe to the jar:

Cinnamon Coffee Cake

1/4 cup shortening
1 egg
1 teaspoon vanilla
1/2 cup milk
2 teaspoons butter
Cinnamon and sugar to taste

Preheat oven to 350 degrees F. Put all ingredients above in a bowl and beat till smooth. Add the contents of the jar and mix well. Pour into 9 inch pie plate and bake for approximately 20 minutes. Take out of oven and spread with butter. Sprinkle sugar and cinnamon over top.

# Peanut Butter Brownie Mix

1 1/4 cup all-purpose flour
1/4 teaspoon salt
1/2 teaspoon baking powder
1/2 cup cocoa
1 cup granulated sugar
1 cup peanut butter chips
Jar – Wide mouth quart glass canning jar

Mix flour, baking powder and salt together in a bowl. Place flour mixture in the jar, pack, and then layer the rest of the ingredients.

 Attach the following recipe to the jar:

Peanut Butter Brownies

1/4 cup corn syrup
1 teaspoon vanilla
2 eggs
3/4 cup butter

Preheat oven to 350 degrees F. Mix all the ingredients above in a large bowl and mix well. Add all the ingredients from jar and stir until well mixed. Bake for 20 to 30 minutes.

*Optional Frosting*
1/2 cup butter
3/4 cup peanut butter
12 oz. semi-sweet chocolate chips

Put all the ingredients above in a microwavable dish and microwave on high for 1 1/2 minutes. Stir until smooth and spread over cooled brownies.

# Breads

## Pumpkin Bread Mix

3 1/2 cups all-purpose flour
2 teaspoons baking soda
1 1/2 teaspoons salt
1 teaspoon cinnamon
1 teaspoon allspice
1 teaspoon nutmeg
1/2 teaspoon ground cloves
Jar – Wide mouth quart glass canning jar

Mix all the ingredients above and put in canning jar.

Attach the following recipe to the jar:

Pumpkin Bread

3 cups granulated sugar
1 cup vegetable oil
4 eggs, beaten
1 lb. canned pumpkin
2/3 cup water

Preheat oven to 350 degrees F. Mix sugar, oil and eggs together. Add can of pumpkin. Add pumpkin bread mix from the jar, then water, stirring until mixed. Pour the batter into 2 greased and floured 9" x 5" loaf pans. Bake for 55 to 60 minutes.

# Nut Bread Mix

2 cups all-purpose flour
4 teaspoons baking powder
1 teaspoon salt
3/4 cup chopped walnuts
Jar – Wide mouth pint glass canning jar

Mix the flour, baking powder and salt together. Place the flour mixture in jar, then the walnuts. Seal the jar.

Attach the following recipe to the jar:

Nut Bread

1 egg, beaten
1 cup sugar
1 cup milk

Preheat oven to 325 degrees F. Mix egg, milk and sugar together in a large bowl. Add the ingredients from the jar. Stir until smooth. Pour into a buttered loaf pan. Bake for about 45 minutes.

# Banana Wheat Bread Mix

*This recipe makes one loaf and fits in a pint canning jar. Use a quart jar if you want to double the recipe.*

2 cups whole wheat flour
1 teaspoon baking soda
1 teaspoon salt
1/2 cup chopped pecans
Jar – Wide mouth pint glass canning jar

Mix all the above ingredients together except pecans. Place flour mixture in jar, then pecans. Seal jar.

Attach the following recipe to the jar:

Banana Wheat Bread

1/2 cup honey
2 eggs, beaten
1/4 cup vegetable oil
3 medium bananas, peeled
1 teaspoon vanilla

Preheat oven to 350 degrees F. Mash bananas in a bowl, and then add the rest of the ingredients above to bananas. Put the contents of the jar in a large bowl, add banana mixture and mix well. Pour into a greased 9" x 5" loaf pan and bake 50 to 60 minutes or until toothpick inserted near the center comes out clean.

# Zucchini Bread Mix

3 cups all-purpose flour
1 teaspoon baking soda
3 teaspoons cinnamon
1 teaspoon salt
1 teaspoon baking powder
1/2 cup chopped walnuts
Jar – Wide mouth quart glass canning jar

Mix all the above ingredients except walnuts. Place all in jar and seal jar.

Attach the following recipe to the jar:

Zucchini Bread

2 cups granulated sugar
2 cups grated zucchini
2 teaspoons vanilla
3 eggs
1 cup vegetable oil

Preheat oven to 325 degrees F. In a large bowl, combine eggs, sugar and oil. Add vanilla and zucchini. Stir in the jar of zucchini bread mix until blended.

Grease and flour 2 8" x 4" loaf pans. Pour batter evenly between the 2 pans. Bake for 55 to 65 minutes.

# Pineapple Bread Mix

*This recipe will make 2 pineapple bread loaves.*

2 cups all-purpose flour
1 teaspoon baking powder
1/2 teaspoon salt
1 teaspoon baking soda
1/2 cup granulated sugar
1 cup raisins
1/2 cup chopped nuts
Jar – Wide mouth quart glass canning jar

Combine flour, baking powder, baking soda and salt. Layer in jar in this order: flour mixture, sugar, nuts, raisins. Seal jar.

Attach the following recipe to the jar:

Pineapple Bread

1 egg, slightly beaten
1 teaspoon vanilla
2 tablespoons melted margarine
1 cup crushed pineapple, well drained

Combine egg, vanilla and margarine in a large bowl. Add the bread mix from the jar. Stir until well blended. Add drained pineapple. Pour into 2 greased loaf pans. Bake 350 degrees for 50 to 60 minutes or until inserted toothpick comes out clean.

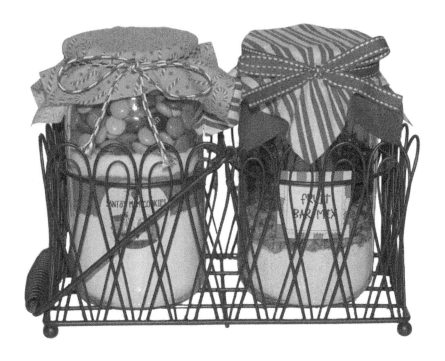

This cute wire canning jar holder with a handle can be found at Walmart. It's perfect for gifting 2 jars.

Exclusively for *100 Easy Recipes In Jars* readers:

Over 2000 Online Labels

and Recipe Cards for the recipes in this book

Available at:

# NorthPoleChristmas.com/jars.html

# 100 More Easy Recipes In Jars

## Bonnie Scott

# 100 More Easy Recipes in Jars

Jars, jars, jars – everyone is hooked on jars today for decorating, storing and organizing. Look at any homemaker blog, the shelves of your local craft store and the big box chain stores and you'll find tons of jars in every shape and size.

100 More Easy Recipes in Jars is the 2$^{nd}$ book in a series to incorporate this latest trend with a delicious homemade gift that's sure to please everyone.

You have an almost unlimited variety of choices when it comes to making gifts in jars. Even if you're not the greatest chef on the block, never fear. With this book you have a wealth of simple and easy recipes that will make your gift giving easy this year.

Whether you're looking for a recipe for a rich and decadent dessert, savory seasoning or warm, satisfying soup, you'll find a variety of recipes for almost any occasion in this latest collection. Use the easy-to-follow directions and add your own creative touch to create a fun and tasty gift. Make up a whole batch and you're ready for any last-minute gift-giving occasion that comes along.

These festive gift jars are great for a favorite teacher, your pastor or a thank-you gift for a helpful neighbor. You'll find many occasions that are just right for gifts in jars, so keep a few handy.

# Filling the Jar

Whether you're using a Mason jar, glass canister or a plastic storage jar, make sure the inside of the jar stays clean as you fill it with your ingredients. You don't want a flour or confectioners sugar coated jar on display, so wipe the inside as you add the layers if there is a mess on the glass.

Just like layered sand art, think about how you will position your layers. A variety in color, texture and thickness adds to the decorative look of your jar.

The contents will settle, so place the finest ground ingredients like flour in the bottom and work up to the coarsest items at the top if you are layering your jar.

Pack your layers to conserve space and create definite layers. Use a bean masher tool or a flat-bottomed glass to tamp down the layers. If you wind up with extra space at the top of the jar, add extra chocolate chips, nuts or other ingredients that are part of the recipe to fill the container to the top.

# Fresh Ingredients

Don't even think about clearing out your pantry to make these gifts! Use only fresh ingredients, as the recipient may not use your recipe right away. Spices lose their flavor, nuts get rancid and items like baking soda and baking powder lose their potency.

Dry mixes will keep 6 to 8 months if stored in a cool, dry place sealed in jar until ready to use.

Some ingredients tend to harden when exposed to the air. Brown sugar is one culprit, and it's popular in many cookie and bar recipes. It's best to either inform the recipient that your recipe should be used within a few weeks or place the brown sugar in a sealed plastic bag.

# Jar Sizes and Capacity

Here are the capacities of standard size canning jars:

Quart = 4 cups or 32 ounces

Pint = 2 cups or 16 ounces

Half pint = 1 cup or 8 ounces

Quarter pint = 1/2 cup or 4 ounces

If you are packing your ingredients tightly, you can fit:

Quart = 4 3/4 cups

Pint = 2 1/8 cups

Half pint = 1 cup + 2 tablespoons

Items like chocolate chips and nuts can't be compressed. If you're using some of these non-packable items and some packable items, the amount your jar will hold will probably fall in between the two amounts above.

Even Ball jars come in various shapes. For example, the pint size Ball jar comes in a squatty format or a tall shape.

You can purchase jars at your local grocery store, Wal-Mart, Target or craft stores. Most craft stores carry a large variety of jars; some jars have a one-piece lid that might be more convenient for storing the seasoning mixes in this book.

# Visual Jar Filling

A canning funnel is inexpensive and will really help in filling the jars without making much of a mess inside the jar. Funnels can be found next to the canning jars in most stores.

The flour mixture is the best layer to put in the jar first because it will pack hard, and since it is so fine and dusty, by being first it won't get all over the chocolate chips or M&M's – layers you want to display cleanly.

Pack the flour layer well with a packing tool – bean masher like this one or the flat bottom of a glass.

Adding a layer like brown sugar creates layering interest for your jar masterpiece and at the same time, it holds the flour where it needs to remain. Measure the brown sugar, packed for the recipe, then unpack it to place it in the jar. Pack it again after it is in the jar.

After all the packable layers have been added, add the items that won't be packed, like chocolate chips, dried fruit and M&M's.

# Hints and Tips

Some people think the jars are so pretty, they won't use them right away. If your jar contains brown sugar and the recipient decides to use the jar after a year, they will have to chisel the brown sugar out.

If the brown sugar does become hard in the jar, after removing it:

- Place the brown sugar in the microwave with a small container of water beside it. Microwave for one minute. Then, check and continue to microwave in 30-second increments until the sugar is soft.

The jars themselves are relatively inexpensive. A case of quart or pint jars is about $15 at Wal-Mart.

Use the small resealable snack bags (6 1/2" x 3 1/4") to add an ingredient to a jar if necessary, found at the Dollar Store.

Book One of *100 Easy Recipes in Jars* has 100 more recipes and 2000 additional labels and recipe cards for jars. Available in both Kindle and paperback versions.

# Get Creative with Containers

Browse around a craft store, hobby store or department store like Wal-Mart or Target for loads of interesting containers to hold your gifts. Think outside the box and surprise your recipient with something for their home as well as for their tummy.

Kitchen utensils and accessories would be thoughtful add-ons for a newlywed couple or someone just starting out in their first apartment. Place your gift jar in a mixing bowl; add some utensils, measuring cups and tea towels for a perfect shower or housewarming gift.

Pack a teapot with ingredients to make almond tea bread or pecan coffee muffins. Add a box of a favorite tea and package it all together on a small serving tray.

Make a basket filled with movie night treats. Include the latest DVD, a jar of your homemade nuts or snacks, a couple packs of microwave popcorn and a container of vanilla hot chocolate. 100 Easy Recipes in Jars book one also has popcorn seasonings to add. Instead of a basket, use an oversized plastic bowl to use when the popcorn is ready to serve.

# Seasoning Mixes

It is really quite cost-effective to make your own seasoning mixes. You can easily save 50% or more on spice mixes by making your own and it's a great way to get the taste you and your family prefer. You can also control the amount of ingredients like salt, MSG, preservatives, dyes and other additives.

Take a look at the spice and seasoning area of your local grocer. It seems that area is always expanding as new brands and flavor combinations keep adding to the number of spices and herbs on the shelves.

If you have a group of ethnic dishes that are always on your short list, create seasoning combinations to make preparing them a snap. Italian, Cajun or Mexican spice combos are ready when you are for quickly seasoning a favorite ethnic dish to perfection. Even everyday dishes like steamed veggies or microwave popcorn get an extra punch of flavor with your own personal style of flavoring.

Creating your own seasoning mixes is an easy way to indulge your creative culinary nature without spending hours bending over a hot stove. It's also far less costly to make up your own secret herb or seasoning recipes. You'll know they are fresh and you can make as much or as little as you choose.

By blending your own seasoning combinations, you can fine-tune each to suit your own taste of sweetness, heat and salt. Strong flavored or spicy seasonings can be tamed down or punched up to suit your family's taste buds. You can even have an adult and a kid-friendly version to please everyone.

To blend the seasonings together well, grind them in a spice or coffee grinder, food processor or use a mortar & pestle. This ensures that all the ingredients are the same size and well incorporated.

You can get great prices on large quantities of herbs and spices at wholesale stores like Costco, BJ's and Sam's Club. However, these are pretty big containers, so you probably should make up a bunch of these seasoning mixes for gifts. Remember, spices and herbs lose their potency rather quickly, so plan to use the spices within six months.

# Fabric Jar Toppers

I usually use 2 pieces of fabric on the top of jars, but just one piece also works nicely. For 2 pieces, I use the placement above. For one fabric, just cut one square. For 2 different fabrics, cut 2 squares.

I use from a 4" square to a 9" square. Use a 6" or 6 1/2" square or even smaller if you want the top layer in a quart jar to be viewable. If the top portion of your quart jar is empty, you might make the squares larger to cover up the empty area. If the jar is a pint or half-pint, I would use a 4" square.

Use a thin brown rubber band about 3" long around the top of the jar over the fabric before adding the trim or ribbon. The rubber band will hold the fabric in place while you add the ribbon. Use approximately 30 inches of ribbon for each jar top.

Thin ribbons about 3/8" work well as ribbons thinner than 3/8". Although if the ribbon is too thin, the rubber band may show through. Also wider ribbon that is translucent and light will work. I have used ribbons like that in this book that are 1 1/2" wide and 1" wide. The ribbon below is 1 1/2" wide.

All the ribbons, trim and fabrics used in this book are available at either Hobby Lobby or Joann Fabric stores.

# Labels, Hang Tags, Recipe Cards

Use the labels and more available at:

## www.NorthPoleChristmas.com/jarsbook2.html

There are at least 2 pages of labels specifically for each recipe in separate pdf files available to print. They can be printed on paper, 2 1/2" white round labels or 2 1/2" round Kraft Brown labels.

The Kraft Brown labels (by Avery) produce a more subdued look to the label because the colors on top of brown won't be as vibrant as the white labels. Some of the labels in the photos in this book were made with the Kraft Brown labels. Use the following Avery labels for these templates:

Avery Kraft Brown 2 1/2" labels #22818

Avery Glossy White 2 1/2" labels #41462

If you don't want to use labels, printing the jar labels on good quality paper works just as well. Cut them out and stick the labels to your jars with double-faced tape.

Since there are 100 recipes in this book and at least 2 pages of labels per recipe, making over 200 pages of labels, there are way too many to include in this book. So the labels are available on the web and can be accessed at www.NorthPoleChristmas.com/jarsbook2.html

# JAR LAYERS

The Jar Layers section includes ingredients that will be layered in jars and the recipient does the actual cooking using the attached recipe.

# BREAD

## Sweet Cornbread Muffins

FILLS ONE QUART GLASS JAR

2 cups all-purpose flour
1 1/2 cups yellow cornmeal
1/2 cup + 2 tablespoons granulated sugar
3 tablespoons baking powder
3/4 teaspoon salt

Combine all ingredients and place in a quart jar. Seal jar.

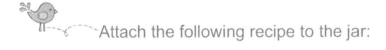Attach the following recipe to the jar:

Sweet Cornbread Muffins

2 tablespoons vegetable oil
1/3 cup milk
1 egg
1 cup cornbread mix from jar

Preheat oven to 400 degrees F. In a medium bowl, combine oil, milk and egg. Add 1 cup of cornbread mix from jar and mix well. Spray an 8x8-inch baking pan or 6 muffin cups with non-stick cooking spray. Pour batter into pan or muffin cups. (Fill muffin cups 2/3 full.) Bake at 400 degrees F for 15 to 17 minutes. Yield: 6 muffins.

# Almond Tea Bread

## FILLS ONE QUART GLASS JAR

2 cups all-purpose flour
1/4 teaspoon baking powder
1/4 teaspoon baking soda
1/4 teaspoon salt
1 cup granulated sugar
1/2 cup slivered almonds

Mix together flour, baking powder, baking soda and salt in a bowl. Layer in quart jar, packing well after each layer: flour mixture then sugar. Place almonds on top. Seal jar.

 Attach the following recipe to the jar:

Almond Tea Bread

1/2 cup butter, softened
1 egg
1/2 cup evaporated milk
1/4 teaspoon almond extract

In a bowl, combine butter, egg, milk and almond extract. Add the contents of the jar and mix well. Pour batter into a greased 9" x 5" loaf pan. Bake at 350 degrees for 1 hour. Cool before serving. Yield: 1 loaf.

# Pumpkin Bread

## FILLS ONE QUART GLASS JAR

1 3/4 cups all-purpose flour
1 teaspoon baking soda
1 teaspoon nutmeg
1 teaspoon cinnamon
3/4 teaspoon salt
1/2 teaspoon baking powder
1/2 teaspoon allspice
1/4 teaspoon ground cloves
1 1/2 cups granulated sugar
1/2 cup pecans, chopped

In a bowl, combine flour, baking soda, nutmeg, cinnamon, salt, baking powder, allspice, and cloves. Place flour mixture in a quart jar, then sugar, packing each layer. Add nuts on top. Seal jar.

 Attach the following recipe to the jar:

Pumpkin Bread
1/3 cup water
1/2 vegetable cup oil
2 eggs, beaten
1 cup pumpkin puree

Preheat oven to 350 degrees F. Grease a 9x5-inch loaf pan. Pour contents of jar in a large bowl. Stir in water and oil. Beat eggs and mix into batter. Blend in the pumpkin. Pour batter into loaf pan. Bake for 1 hour or until passes toothpick test. Cool 5 minutes in pan before removing. Yield: 1 loaf.

# Banana Nut Bread

## FILLS ONE QUART GLASS JAR

2 cups all-purpose flour
1/8 teaspoon salt
1 teaspoon baking soda
1/2 teaspoon baking powder
1 cup granulated sugar
1/2 cup chopped nuts

Mix together flour, salt, baking soda and baking powder in a bowl. Layer in quart jar, packing well: flour mixture, sugar, then add nuts on top. Seal jar.

Attach the following recipe to the jar:

Banana Nut Bread

3 bananas
1/2 cup oil
2 eggs, beaten
3 tablespoons milk
1/2 teaspoon vanilla

In a large bowl, mash 3 bananas. Add oil, eggs, milk and vanilla; mix well. Pour contents of the jar into the bowl and beat well. Pour into a greased and floured loaf pan and bake at 350 degrees F for 1 hour. Yield: 1 loaf.

# Raisin Bread

## FILLS ONE QUART GLASS JAR

3 cups all-purpose flour
3 teaspoons baking powder
2 teaspoons ground cinnamon
1 teaspoon salt
1/2 teaspoon baking soda
1/2 cup granulated sugar
1 1/4 cup raisins

In a bowl, combine flour, baking powder, cinnamon, salt and baking soda. Place flour mixture in quart jar, then sugar, packing each layer. Place raisins in a small resealable plastic bag and add to jar on top of sugar. Seal jar.

Attach the following recipe to the jar:

Raisin Bread

1 egg
1/4 cup butter, melted
1/2 cup applesauce
1 cup milk

Preheat oven to 350 degrees F. Grease a 9x5x3 inch loaf pan. Pour contents of the jar in a large bowl. Make a well in the center. In another bowl, beat egg, mix in butter, applesauce and milk. Pour into well. Stir just enough to moisten. Pour into loaf pan.
Bake at 350 degrees F for 55 to 60 minutes. Yield: 1 loaf.

# Lemon Nut Bread

## FILLS ONE QUART GLASS JAR

1 1/2 cups all-purpose flour
1/2 teaspoon salt
1 teaspoon baking powder
1 cup granulated sugar
1/2 cup chopped walnuts

In a bowl, combine flour, salt and baking powder. Place flour mixture in quart jar, then sugar, packing each layer. Add nuts on top. Seal jar.

Attach the following recipe to the jar:

Lemon Nut Bread

6 tablespoons butter, melted
2 eggs
1/2 cup milk
1 teaspoon lemon zest

*Glaze:*
1/2 cup granulated sugar
1 lemon, juiced

In a large bowl, mix butter and eggs together. Add milk and contents of jar; mix well. Stir in grated lemon zest. Pour batter in a greased and floured 9x5-inch loaf pan. Bake at 350 degrees F for 1 hour. Allow bread to cool in the pan for 5 minutes.

*Glaze:*

Combine sugar and the juice of a lemon. Remove bread from pan. Pour glaze over warm bread.

# Cherry Bread

## FILLS ONE QUART GLASS JAR

1 1/2 cups all-purpose flour
1 1/2 teaspoons baking powder
1 cup granulated sugar
3/4 cup nuts, chopped

Mix flour and baking powder. Place flour mixture in jar, then sugar, packing each layer. Add nuts on top. Seal jar.

Attach the following recipe to the jar:

Cherry Bread

2 eggs, well beaten
1 5 ounce jar maraschino cherries cut up – juice and all

In a large bowl, combine the eggs and cherries with cherry juice. Add the contents of the jar and mix well. Bake in a well-greased 9 x 5 inch pan at 350 degrees F for 1 hour.

Yield: 1 loaf.

# BARS

## Dual Chip Bars

### FILLS ONE QUART GLASS JAR

1 1/2 cups graham cracker crumbs (about 24 squares)
2 cups semisweet chocolate chips
1 cup peanut butter chips

Place graham cracker crumbs in a small resealable plastic bag. In a quart jar, place chocolate chips and peanut butter chips. Add the bag of graham crackers on top. Seal jar.

 Attach the following recipe to the jar:

Dual Chip Bars

1/2 cup butter
1 can (14 oz.) sweetened condensed milk

Preheat oven to 350 degrees F. Put butter in a 13x9x2-inch baking pan; place pan in oven until melted. Remove from oven. Remove graham cracker crumbs from jar and sprinkle crumbs evenly over butter.  Pour milk uniformly over crumbs. Sprinkle the remaining contents of jar over milk; press down firmly.  Bake at 350 degrees F for 25 to 30 minutes or until golden brown.  Cool on wire rack before cutting.

# Deep Dish Brownies

## FILLS ONE PINT GLASS JAR

*This recipe makes brownies that taste like store-bought prepared mixes ... only richer! These brownies get an A+ all around for taste and ease of cooking.*

3/4 cup all-purpose flour
1/2 teaspoon baking powder
1/2 teaspoon salt
1/2 cup cocoa
1 cup granulated sugar

Mix together flour, baking powder and salt in a bowl. Layer in pint jar: flour mixture, cocoa, sugar. Pack well after each layer. Seal jar.

Attach the following recipe to the jar:

Deep Dish Brownies

3/4 cup butter, melted
1 1/2 teaspoons vanilla
1/2 cup granulated sugar
3 eggs

Preheat oven to 350 degrees F. Blend melted butter, vanilla and sugar in a mixing bowl. Add eggs, beat well with a spoon. Gradually add contents of jar to egg mixture and stir until blended well. Spread in greased 8" square pan. Bake at 350 degrees F for 40 minutes. Cool and cut into squares.

# Chewy Butterscotch Brownies

## FILLS ONE QUART GLASS JAR

1 1/4 cups all-purpose flour
1/2 teaspoon baking powder
1/4 teaspoon salt
1 cup brown sugar, packed
3/4 cup butterscotch-flavored morsels
1/2 cup pecans or walnuts, chopped
plus
1 cup butterscotch-flavored morsels for frosting

Mix flour, baking powder and salt together in a bowl. Place flour mixture in a jar, pack. Then add brown sugar and pack. Add 3/4 cup butterscotch morsels, then nuts, then remaining butterscotch morsels on top. (Be sure to put the butterscotch morsels for the frosting on top, so they can be removed from the jar easily by the recipient.) Seal jar.

 Attach the following recipe to the jar:

Frosted Butterscotch Brownies

1/2 cup butter, softened
1 tablespoon vanilla extract
2 eggs

Preheat oven to 350 degrees F. Remove the top layer of butterscotch-flavored morsels from the jar (down to the nuts) and set aside. These will be used for frosting.

Mix butter and vanilla extract in a large bowl until creamy. Add eggs and beat well. Pour remainder of the jar contents into the bowl and mix until well blended. Pour the mixture into a lightly greased 13x9 inch baking pan. Bake for 30 minutes or until inserted toothpick comes out clean.

Frosting - Butterscotch Glaze:

3/4 cup butterscotch-flavored morsels (from jar)
2 tablespoons water
2 tablespoons granulated sugar
1 1/2 teaspoons light corn syrup

Bring corn syrup, water and sugar to a boil in a pan over medium-high heat. Remove from heat and add reserved butterscotch-flavored chips. Stir until all butterscotch chips are melted. Pour glaze over brownies and spread evenly. Let cool before cutting.

# Easy Chocolate Brownies

### FILLS ONE QUART GLASS JAR

2 cups biscuit baking mix
1 cup coarsely chopped nuts
1 (12 oz.) pkg. semi-sweet chocolate chips

Pack the biscuit mix, nuts and chocolate chips in a quart jar. Be sure to put chocolate chips on top so 1 cup of the chocolate can be removed easily. (Or put 1 cup of the chocolate chips in a small resealable plastic bag and label as 1 cup.) Seal jar.

 Attach the following recipe to the jar:

Easy Chocolate Brownies

1/4 cup margarine
1 (14 oz.) can sweetened condensed milk
1 egg, beaten
1 teaspoon vanilla
Confectioners sugar

Preheat oven to 350 degrees F. Remove 1 cup of chocolate chips from jar. In a large saucepan over low heat, melt margarine and 1 cup chocolate chips from the jar together; remove from heat. Add milk, egg, vanilla and remainder of ingredients from the jar. Pour into well-greased 13x9" baking pan. Bake 20 to 25 minutes or until brownies begin to pull away from sides of pan. Cool. Sprinkle with confectioners sugar. Makes 2 dozen brownies.

# Peanut Butter Chocolate Bars

## FILLS ONE QUART GLASS JAR

1 cup all-purpose flour
1/4 teaspoon salt
1 1/4 cups granulated sugar
1 (11 oz.) pkg. chocolate chips

Mix flour and salt together. Put flour mixture in jar and pack. Add sugar, then chocolate chips. (Place chocolate chips on top so the recipient can remove 3/4 cup easily.) Seal jar.

 Attach the following recipe to the jar:

Peanut Butter Chocolate Bars

1 cup peanut butter
6 tablespoons butter, softened
3 eggs
1 teaspoon vanilla

Preheat oven to 350 degrees F. Remove 3/4 cup of chocolate chips from jar; set aside. In large bowl, beat butter and peanut butter until smooth, about 1 minute. Add eggs and vanilla; beat until well mixed and creamy. Mix in remaining contents of jar.
Spread in an ungreased 13x9" pan. Bake at 350 degrees F 25 to 30 minutes or until edges begin to turn brown. Remove from oven and immediately sprinkle remaining chocolate chips over cookie layer. Let stand 5 minutes; spread chocolate evenly over top. Cut into bars.

# Chewy Granola Bars

## FILLS ONE QUART GLASS JAR

2/3 cup brown sugar
2 cups quick oats
1/4 cup wheat germ
1/3 cup sunflower seeds
2/3 cup nuts, chopped
1/3 cup raisins or dried cherries

Layer in order listed in a quart jar, packing the first 3 layers well. Raisins or cherries can be put in a resealable plastic bag (to preserve freshness) and added on top of nuts. Seal jar.

Attach the following recipe to the jar:

Chewy Granola Bars

1/3 cup butter, melted
1/3 cup light corn syrup
1/2 cup peanut butter
2 teaspoons vanilla

Preheat oven to 350 degrees F. In a large bowl, mix butter, corn syrup, peanut butter and vanilla together. Add contents of jar and mix well. Press into an 8x8-inch or 9x9-inch pan. Bake at 350 degrees F for 15 to 20 minutes.

# Egg-Less Cocoa Crazy Cake

## FILLS ONE QUART GLASS JAR

1 3/4 cups all-purpose flour
1 teaspoon baking soda
1/4 teaspoon salt
1 cup granulated sugar
3 tablespoons unsweetened cocoa

Mix flour, baking soda and salt together. Put flour mixture in jar and pack. Mix sugar and cocoa together. Add sugar mixture to jar and pack. Seal jar.

Attach the following recipe to the jar:

Egg-Less Cocoa Crazy Cake

1 teaspoon vanilla
1 tablespoon vinegar
5 tablespoons butter, melted
1 cup water
Confectioners' sugar (optional)

Pour the contents of the jar into a bowl. Make 3 wells in the dry ingredients. Pour vanilla in 1 well, vinegar in another, and melted butter in the third. Pour water over all and beat with a spoon until well blended. Pour into greased 9" square pan and bake at 350 degrees F for 25 minutes. When cool, sprinkle with confectioners' sugar or frost.

221

# S'more Brownies

## FILLS ONE QUART GLASS JAR

*Be sure to use small plastic snack bags for packing so they all fit in the jar.*

1/2 cup and 2 tablespoons all-purpose flour
1/2 teaspoon baking powder
1/2 teaspoon salt
1/3 cup unsweetened cocoa powder
1 cup and 2 tablespoons granulated sugar
2 graham crackers
3 (1.5 oz.) milk chocolate bars
3/4 cup miniature marshmallows
3 small resealable snack bags (6 1/2" x 3 1/4")

Combine flour, baking powder and salt. Put in quart jar and pack firmly. Add cocoa powder as the next layer and pack. Add sugar and pack firmly.

Break graham crackers into small pieces and place in a small resealable snack bag. Break each chocolate bar into about 16 pieces and place in another snack bag. In the final snack bag, add marshmallows. Squeeze as much air as possible out of each snack bag.

Cut a double layer of wax paper to fit inside the jar and lay it on top of the last sugar layer. Now add the graham cracker bag, chocolate bag and marshmallow bag to the jar. Seal jar.

 Attach the following recipe to the jar:

S'more Brownies

6 tablespoons butter or margarine
2 eggs, slightly beaten

Preheat oven to 350 degrees F. Remove the 3 plastic bags from inside the jar and set aside. Remove the wax paper from the jar and empty the ingredients of the jar into a large bowl. Add butter or margarine and eggs. Mix until well blended.

Spray an 8" or 9" square baking dish with non-stick cooking spray. Pour batter into pan and spread evenly. Bake at 350 degrees F. for 20 minutes. Remove, sprinkle the contents of each plastic bag on top of the brownie and bake for 10 minutes more. Allow to cool before cutting into squares.

# Noel Bars

## FILLS ONE PINT GLASS JAR

1/3 cup all-purpose flour
1/8 teaspoon baking soda
1/8 teaspoon salt
1 cup brown sugar
1/2 to 3/4 cup chopped nuts

Combine flour, salt and baking soda in bowl. Put in jar and pack. Add brown sugar and pack. Add nuts on top. Seal jar.

Attach the following recipe to the jar:

Noel Bars

2 tablespoons butter
2 eggs, beaten
1 teaspoon vanilla
Confectioners' sugar
Green icing

Preheat oven to 350 degrees F. Melt butter in 9x9x2inch pan. Pour contents of jar in a bowl. Add eggs and vanilla; mix well. Carefully pour batter over butter in pan. Do not stir.

Bake at 350 degrees F for 20 to 25 minutes. Remove from oven and sprinkle with confectioners' sugar. Invert onto wax paper on a rack immediately. When cool, cut into long bars and write "Noel" in green icing on confectioners' sugar side.

# Pecan Coffee Muffins

## FILLS ONE QUART GLASS JAR

1 cup pecans
1 3/4 cups all-purpose flour
1/4 teaspoon salt
3 teaspoons baking powder
1/2 cup dark brown sugar, firmly packed

Coarsely chop pecans. In a large bowl, combine flour, salt and baking powder. Put flour mixture in quart jar, then brown sugar, packing each layer. Add pecans on top. Seal jar.

Attach the following recipe to the jar:

Pecan Coffee Muffins

1 egg
1/2 cup milk
1/2 cup butter, melted
2 teaspoons strong cold coffee
1 teaspoon vanilla

Line 12 muffin cups with cupcake liners or spray lightly with non-stick cooking spray. In a large bowl, lightly beat egg. Add milk, butter, coffee and vanilla to the egg; blend well. Add contents of the jar; mix just until combined. Spoon mixture into buttered muffin cups. Bake at 400 degrees F for 16 to 20 minutes or until inserted toothpick comes out clean. Yield: 12 muffins.

# Double Chocolate Cupcakes

## FILLS ONE QUART GLASS JAR

*Fit these ingredients into a quart jar and there will be enough room at the top of the jar to add some cupcake liners.*

1 1/2 cups all-purpose flour
1/2 cup granulated sugar
1/4 cup unsweetened cocoa
1 teaspoon baking soda
1/2 teaspoon salt
1/3 cup semi-sweet chocolate mini morsels

Combine flour, sugar, cocoa, baking soda and salt in a medium bowl. Put in quart jar and pack firmly. Add chocolate mini morsels on top. Seal jar. (Note: There really isn't enough quantity-wise of the sugar and cocoa to make a layer that will show, so just mix all the ingredients together.)

Attach the following recipe to the jar:

Double Chocolate Cupcakes

1/2 cup unsweetened orange juice
1/3 cup water
3 tablespoons vegetable oil
1 tablespoon vinegar
1 teaspoon vanilla
1 teaspoon confectioners' sugar

Pour the contents of the jar in a bowl; make a well in center. Combine orange juice, water, oil, vinegar, and vanilla; add to dry ingredients, stirring until just moistened.

Pour batter in muffin pans lined with cupcake liners, filling 2/3 full. Bake at 375 degrees F for 12 minutes or until a toothpick inserted in center comes out clean. Remove from pans and cool on rack. Sprinkle with confectioners' sugar. Yield: 12 servings.

# Ginger Spice Muffins

## FILLS ONE QUART GLASS JAR

3 1/2 cups all-purpose flour
1/4 cup granulated sugar
2 tablespoons baking powder
1 teaspoon baking soda
2 teaspoons ground cinnamon
1 teaspoon ground nutmeg
1/2 teaspoon ground ginger
1/2 teaspoon ground cloves
1 teaspoon salt

Combine all the ingredients in a bowl. Put in quart jar; pack well. Seal jar.

Attach the following recipe to the jar:

Ginger Spice Muffins

1/2 cup butter or margarine, melted
2 eggs
2 teaspoons vanilla
2 cups milk

Preheat oven to 400 degrees F. Grease 24 muffin tins or use paper liners. In a large bowl, mix butter, eggs, vanilla and milk, then add the contents of the jar. Stir mixture just until the ingredients are well mixed; batter will be lumpy. Pour into muffin pans, filling 2/3 full and bake for 15 minutes at 400 degrees F. Yield: 2 dozen.

# Crumb Muffins

## FILLS ONE QUART GLASS JAR

1 1/2 cups all-purpose flour
1 teaspoon baking powder
1 teaspoon baking soda
1/2 teaspoon salt
3/4 cup granulated sugar

Crumb topping:
1/3 cup packed brown sugar
2 tablespoons all-purpose flour
1/8 teaspoon ground cinnamon

Combine flour, baking powder, baking soda and salt in a bowl. Put in quart jar; pack. Add granulated sugar on top and pack. Mix crumb topping ingredients together and place in a resealable small plastic bag; label the bag. Put on top in quart jar. Seal jar.

Attach the following recipe to the jar:

Crumb Muffins

3 bananas, mashed
1 egg, lightly beaten
1/3 cup butter, melted

1 tablespoon butter, softened

Preheat oven to 375 degrees F. Line ten muffin cups with cupcake liners or spray lightly with non-stick cooking spray. Remove the bag from the top of the jar; set aside.

In a large bowl, beat together bananas, egg and melted butter. Add the contents of the jar (except for topping in bag) and stir just until combined well. Fill muffin cups 2/3 full with batter.

Bake at 375 degrees F for 18 to 20 minutes or until a toothpick inserted comes out clean.

*Topping:*
In a small bowl, pour contents of topping bag. Mix in 1 tablespoon softened butter until well mixed. Sprinkle mixture on top of muffins.

# Brownies in a Jar

## FILLS ONE QUART GLASS JAR

1 cup all-purpose flour
1/2 teaspoon baking powder
1/4 teaspoon salt
1 1/2 cups granulated sugar
1/3 cups Hershey's unsweetened cocoa
1/2 cups mini semi-sweet chocolate chips
1 cup peanut butter chips or white chocolate chips

Mix flour, baking powder and salt together. Put flour mixture in a quart jar and pack. Mix sugar and cocoa together. Add sugar mixture to jar and pack. Add mini chocolate chips next, then peanut butter or white chips. Seal jar.

 Attach the following recipe to the jar:

Brownies

1/2 cup butter, softened
2 eggs, slightly beaten

Preheat oven to 350 degrees F. Empty brownie mix from jar into a large bowl. Add butter and eggs. Gently stir to combine. Spread in a greased and floured 8-inch square baking pan. Bake at 350 degrees F for 35 minutes. Cool in pan. Cut into bars.

# COOKIES & CANDY

*Most of the cookie recipes yield about 24 cookies, give or take a few depending on the ingredients in the jar and the size of the cookie.*

## Christmas Cookies

### FILLS ONE QUART GLASS JAR

*This recipe can also be cut in half and put into pint jars. Regular Rice Krispies and chocolate chips or other flavor chips, like peanut butter, may be used in place of Cocoa Krispies and white chocolate chips.*

1 1/2 cups all-purpose flour
3/4 teaspoon baking soda
1/4 teaspoon baking powder
1/4 cup granulated sugar
1/2 cup packed brown sugar
1/2 cup rolled oats (also called old fashioned oats)
1/2 cup red & green M&M's
1/2 cup cocoa crisped-rice cereal
1/2 cup white chocolate chips

In a bowl, combine flour, baking soda and baking powder. Layer in quart jar in this order: flour mixture, sugar, brown sugar and rolled oats. Pack well after each layer. On top of packed layers, lay M&M's, cereal and chocolate chips. Seal jar.

Attach the following recipe to the jar:

Christmas Cookies

1/2 cup butter
1/2 teaspoon vanilla extract
1 egg

Cream butter, vanilla and egg in a large bowl. Add the contents of the jar and stir until well blended (expect the mix to be dry, but add a few tablespoons of water, if necessary, to combine). Drop by rounded tablespoons on an ungreased cookie sheet. Bake at 350 degrees for 10 to 12 minutes.

# Cranberry White Chocolate Cookies

## FILLS ONE QUART GLASS JAR

1 + 1/8 cups all-purpose flour
1/2 teaspoon salt
1/2 teaspoon baking soda
1/3 cup brown sugar, packed
1/3 cup granulated sugar
1/2 cup rolled oats
1/2 cup dried cranberries
1/2 cup vanilla flavored baking chips
1/2 cup chopped pecans

In a bowl, mix flour, salt and baking soda. In a quart jar, layer ingredients in this order: flour mixture, brown sugar, granulated sugar, and oats, packing firmly after adding each layer. Place cranberries, baking chips and pecans on top. Seal jar.

 Attach the following recipe to the jar:

Cranberry White Chocolate Chip Cookies

1/2 cup softened butter
1 egg
1 teaspoon vanilla

Preheat oven to 350 degrees F. Grease a cookie sheet or line with parchment paper. In a bowl, beat together butter, egg and vanilla until creamy. Add the contents of jar and stir by hand until well mixed. Drop by heaping spoonful on a cookie sheet, about 2 inches apart. Bake at 350 degrees F for 8 to 10 minutes. Yield: 18 cookies.

# Cocoa Peanut Butter Cookie Mix

## FILLS ONE QUART GLASS JAR

*Clean the inside of the jar with a dry paper towel after adding the confectioners' sugar.*

1 1/2 cups all-purpose flour
1 teaspoon baking powder
1/4 teaspoon salt
1 cup packed brown sugar
1 1/2 cups confectioners' sugar
3/4 cups cocoa powder

In a bowl, mix together flour, baking powder and salt. Layer ingredients in a quart jar in this order: flour mixture, brown sugar, confectioners' sugar and cocoa powder. Pack each layer firmly because it will be a tight fit. Seal jar.

Attach the following recipe to the jar:

Cocoa Peanut Butter Cookies

1/2 cup butter, softened
1/2 cup creamy peanut butter
1 egg, slightly beaten
1 teaspoon vanilla

Empty the contents of the jar into a large bowl and mix well. Add butter, peanut butter, egg and vanilla to the bowl. Mix until well blended. Form into 1 1/4 inch balls and place a few inches apart on a parchment lined cookie sheet. Press each cookie down with a fork. Bake at 350 degrees F for 9 to 11 minutes, until edges are browned. Cool 5 minutes on cookie sheet, then transfer to a cooling rack to finish cooling. Yield: 3 dozen cookies.

# Orange Cookie Mix

FILLS ONE QUART GLASS JAR

1 3/4 cups all-purpose flour
1/2 teaspoon baking soda
1/2 teaspoon baking powder
1/2 cup Tang orange powdered drink mix
3/4 cup granulated sugar
1 1/2 cups vanilla flavored baking chips

In a bowl, mix flour, baking soda and baking powder. In a quart jar, layer ingredients in this order: flour mixture, Tang and sugar. Pack firmly after each addition. Lay baking chips on top. Seal jar.

 Attach the following recipe to the jar:

Orange Cookies

1/2 cup butter or margarine, softened
1 egg
1 teaspoon vanilla

Pour the contents of the jar into a bowl; mix well. Add butter, egg and vanilla; stir until well blended. Shape into one inch balls. Bake at 375 degrees F for 12 to 13 minutes, until tops are lightly browned. Yield: 2 1/2 dozen.

# Chocolate Reindeer Droppings

## FILLS ONE QUART GLASS JAR

2/3 cup coconut
2 cups quick oats
1 1/3 cups granulated sugar
1/4 cup cocoa

Place in jar in this order: coconut, quick oats, sugar, cocoa. It may be easier for removal if the sugar and cocoa are placed in resealable small plastic bags and added to the top of the jar. Seal jar.

Attach the following recipe to the jar:

Chocolate Reindeer Droppings

1/3 cup milk
1/3 cup butter

In a pan, boil milk, butter, and from the jar - cocoa and sugar. Remove from heat and add in the remainder of the jar ingredients. Mix well and drop by spoonful on wax paper. Refrigerate.

# Chocolate Walnut Cookies

## FILLS ONE QUART GLASS JAR

1 cup all-purpose flour
1/2 teaspoon baking powder
1 teaspoon salt
1 cup granulated sugar
1 cup chopped walnuts
3 squares unsweetened chocolate

Mix together flour, baking powder and salt in a bowl. Layer in quart jar: flour mixture, sugar, walnuts. Pack well after each layer. Add the 3 squares of chocolate on top. Seal jar.

Attach the following recipe to the jar:

Chocolate Walnut Cookies

1/2 cups butter, melted
2 eggs
3 teaspoons vanilla

Remove the 3 squares of chocolate from the jar and melt in microwave. In a large bowl, combine melted chocolate, butter, eggs and vanilla. Add contents of the jar and mix well. Roll into small balls. Bake at 350 degrees F 8 to 10 minutes.

# Apricot Chews

## FILLS ONE QUART GLASS JAR

1 cup dried apricots (measured after chopping)
1 tablespoon granulated sugar
1 tablespoon flour
2 cups chopped pecans

Put sugar and flour in the quart jar. Add pecans. Add dried apricots on top. (Placing apricots in a small resealable plastic bag for freshness is optional.) Seal jar.

 Attach the following recipe to the jar:

Apricot Chews

1 cup Eagle Brand condensed milk
2 tablespoons lemon juice

Pour the contents of the jar in a bowl. Add condensed milk and lemon juice; mix well. (The mixture will be thin and needs frequent stirring.) Drop on well-greased cookie sheet in small spoonfuls. Bake at 300 degrees for 20 minutes. Remove immediately from pan. Yield: 2 dozen.

# Brownie Bark Cookies

## FILLS ONE PINT GLASS JAR

*This recipe fits in a pint jar. The following picture shows the short pint Bell jar with a 5" square of fabric on top.*

1 cup all-purpose flour
1 teaspoon baking powder
1/8 teaspoon salt
1 cup granulated sugar
2 squares unsweetened baking chocolate bar

Mix together flour, baking powder and salt in a bowl. Layer in pint jar: flour mixture, then sugar. Pack well after each layer. Lay the chocolate squares on top. Seal jar.

Attach the following recipe to the jar:

Brownie Bark Cookies

1/4 cup butter
2 eggs, beaten
1 teaspoon vanilla
Confectioners' sugar

Remove the 2 squares of chocolate from the jar. Melt butter and chocolate squares together. Pour remaining contents of jar in a bowl; mix in eggs and vanilla. Add chocolate mixture and beat well.

On a cookie sheet sprayed with non-stick cooking spray, drop dough by very small (1/2") spoonfuls (dough will spread while baking). Sprinkle with confectioners' sugar. Bake at 350 degrees F for 12 minutes. Yield: Makes: 3 to 4 dozen.

# Chocolate Clusters

## FILLS ONE QUART GLASS JAR

1 cup peanut butter chips
1 cup chocolate chips
1 cup butterscotch chips
3/4 cup unsalted peanuts or chopped walnuts

Layer each cup of chips in a quart jar (don't pack); place nuts in a small resealable plastic bag and put bag on top of chips. Seal jar.

Attach the following recipe to the jar:

Chocolate Clusters

Remove bag of nuts from jar and set aside. Pour the remainder of the jar into a microwave-safe bowl and melt on Medium until melted. Stir occasionally. Watch carefully; don't overcook, just melt. Stir in nuts from bag. Drop candy onto waxed paper and refrigerate.

# Pecan Puffs

## FILLS ONE QUART GLASS JAR

1/4 cup confectioners' sugar
2 cups all-purpose flour
1 cup chopped pecans

Place the ingredients in a quart jar in order listed above, packing well after the first 2 layers. Seal jar.

Attach the following recipe to the jar:

Pecan Puffs

1 cup butter, melted
2 tablespoons vanilla
1 tablespoon water
Confectioners' sugar

Pour the contents of the jar in a bowl. Add butter, vanilla, and water; mix well. Form small 1 inch balls. Bake on ungreased cookie sheet at 300 degrees F for 15 to 20 minutes or until bottoms are delicately browned. While hot, roll in confectioners' sugar. Yield: 3 dozen.

# M&M Cookies

### FILLS ONE QUART GLASS JAR

2 cups all-purpose flour
1 teaspoon salt
1 teaspoon baking soda
1/2 cup granulated sugar
1 cup brown sugar
1 to 1 1/4 cups M&M's

Mix together flour, salt and baking soda in a bowl. Layer in quart jar: flour mixture, brown sugar and sugar. Pack well after each layer. Add M&M's on top of sugar. Seal jar.

 Attach the following recipe to the jar:

M&M Cookies

1 cup butter, melted
2 teaspoons vanilla
2 eggs

Remove M&M's from the jar and set aside. Blend butter, vanilla and eggs; mix well. Add the remaining contents of the jar and mix well. Add 3/4 cup M&M's. Drop by spoonful on ungreased cookie sheet. Slightly push a few of the remaining M&M's on each cookie before baking. Bake at 350 degrees F for 10 minutes.

# Butterscotch-Oatmeal Cookie Mix

## FILLS ONE QUART GLASS JAR

1 cup all-purpose flour
1 teaspoon baking soda
1/8 teaspoon salt
2 cups quick cooking oats
3/4 cup granulated sugar
3/4 cup butterscotch chips

Mix together flour, baking soda and salt in a bowl. Layer in quart jar in this order, packing well after each layer: flour mixture, oats, sugar, then lay butterscotch chips on top (optionally the butterscotch chips can be placed in a small resealable plastic bag and added to the top of the jar). Seal jar.

Attach the following recipe to the jar:

Butterscotch-Oatmeal Cookies

3/4 cup butter

Preheat oven to 350 degrees F. Carefully remove butterscotch chips from the top of the jar. Melt butter and butterscotch chips together in a small saucepan over low heat.

Pour contents of the jar into a bowl; add butterscotch chip mixture. Mix until well blended. Drop by spoonfuls on an ungreased cookie sheet. Bake 10 minutes at 350 degrees F. Cookies will be crisp.

# Crisp Sugar Drop Cookies

## FILLS ONE QUART GLASS JAR

2 1/2 cups al-purpose flour
1/2 teaspoon baking soda
1 teaspoon salt
1 cup granulated sugar

Combine flour, baking soda and salt. Place in quart jar. Add sugar to jar. Seal jar.

Attach the following recipe to the jar:

Crisp Sugar Drop Cookies

1 egg, beaten
2 tablespoons vinegar
1 1/2 teaspoons lemon juice
1 teaspoon vanilla
1/2 cup butter, melted

Combine egg, vinegar, lemon juice, vanilla and butter. Add contents of jar and mix well. Drop by spoonful on an ungreased cookie sheet and flatten with a fork. Bake at 400 degrees F for 10 to 12 minutes.

Optional: For half chocolate-dipped cookies, melt chocolate chips in microwave. Dip the cookie in the chocolate, let drip then dry on wax paper.

# Raisin-Nut Drops

## FILLS ONE QUART GLASS JAR

1 (6 oz.) package semi-sweet chocolate chips
1 cup peanuts
1 cup seedless raisins

Layer each ingredient above in a quart jar. The raisins optionally can be put in a small resealable plastic bag to keep them fresh. Seal jar.

Attach the following recipe to the jar:

Raisin-Nut Drops

Place chocolate, peanuts and raisins in a 2-1/2 quart casserole dish. Cook in microwave for 1 to 3 minutes on HIGH until chocolate chips melt (watch carefully). Stir to cover peanuts and raisins completely. Drop by spoonful onto waxed paper. Place in refrigerator to set.

# Butterscotch Cookies

### FILLS ONE QUART GLASS JAR

1 1/8 cups all-purpose flour
1/2 teaspoon baking soda
1/4 teaspoon baking powder
1/4 teaspoon salt
1/2 cup flaked coconut
1/2 cup brown sugar, packed
1/2 cup granulated sugar
3/4 cup high protein crisp rice and wheat cereal (Special-K)
3/4 cup butterscotch chips
1/2 cup pecans, chopped

Mix flour, baking soda, baking powder and salt together. Put flour mixture in jar and pack. Layer coconut, brown sugar and granulated sugar in jar, packing each layer well. On top, place Special-K, butterscotch chips and pecans. Seal jar.

 Attach the following recipe to the jar:

Butterscotch Cookies

1/2 cup butter, softened
1 egg
1/2 teaspoon vanilla

Preheat oven to 350 degrees F. Empty cookie mix from jar into a large bowl. Add butter, egg and vanilla, and mix well. Roll into 1 1/2" balls. Place on ungreased cookie sheets, then flatten each cookie ball. Bake for 8 to 10 minutes. Yield: 2 dozen.

# Raisin Spice Cookies

## FILLS ONE QUART GLASS JAR

1 cup all-purpose flour
1 teaspoon ground cinnamon
1 teaspoon baking soda
1/2 teaspoon ground nutmeg
1/2 teaspoon salt
3/4 cup brown sugar, packed
1/2 cup granulated sugar
2 cups rolled oats
1/2 cup raisins

In a bowl, mix flour, cinnamon, baking soda, nutmeg and salt. In a quart jar, layer ingredients in this order: flour mixture, brown sugar, granulated sugar, rolled oats. Pack firmly after each addition. Optionally, place raisins in a small resealable plastic bag and lay on top in the jar or just add raisins on top. Seal jar.

Attach the following recipe to the jar:

Raisin Spice Cookies

3/4 cup butter or margarine, softened
1 egg, slightly beaten
1 teaspoon of vanilla

Preheat oven to 350 degrees F. Empty cookie mix from jar into a large bowl. Add butter or margarine, egg and vanilla; mix well. Shape into 1 1/2" balls. Place on a greased or parchment lined cookie sheet, 2 inches apart. Bake for 11 to 13 minutes. Yield: 2 dozen.

# Million Dollar Cookie Mix

## FILLS ONE QUART GLASS JAR

2 cups all-purpose flour
1/2 teaspoon salt
1/2 teaspoon baking soda
1/2 cup brown sugar
1/2 cup granulated sugar
1/2 cup chopped nuts

Mix flour, salt and baking soda together. Put flour mixture in jar and pack. Layer brown sugar, then granulated sugar in a quart jar, packing each layer well. On top, place nuts. Seal jar.

Attach the following recipe to the jar:

Million Dollar Cookies

1 cup butter
1 teaspoon vanilla
1 egg
Granulated sugar

Pour contents of jar into a large bowl. Add butter, vanilla and egg. Mix and roll into small balls. Roll each ball in granulated sugar. Place on greased or parchment lined cookie sheet. Flatten each with the bottom of a small glass dipped in sugar. Bake at 350 degrees F for 10 minutes.

# OATMEAL

## Baked Oatmeal

### FILLS ONE QUART GLASS JAR

*There is enough room at the top of this quart jar to add some nuts or raisins in a small resealable plastic bag if you wish.*

3 cups quick cooking oats
1 tablespoon baking powder
1/2 teaspoon salt
2 tablespoons brown sugar
1/2 teaspoon cinnamon
3/4 cup granulated sugar

Put oats in a quart jar and pack. In a small bowl, mix together baking powder, salt, brown sugar and cinnamon. Add to jar as the next layer. Pour granulated sugar on top. Seal jar.

Attach the following recipe to the jar:

Baked Oatmeal

1/2 cup applesauce or vegetable oil
2 eggs
1 cup milk

Optional – 1/2 cup chopped almonds or walnuts, coconut, diced apples, raisins, blueberries, diced peaches or a can of fruit.

Combine applesauce or oil, eggs and milk; beat well. Add the contents of the jar and stir until well mixed. Add any of the optional ingredients above. Pour into a lightly greased 8" or 9" cake pan. Sprinkle cinnamon and brown sugar on top, if desired. Refrigerate overnight.

The next morning, preheat oven to 350 degrees F. Bake for 35 minutes or until oatmeal is firm. Serve with milk.

# Low Fat Oatmeal

## FILLS ONE PINT GLASS JAR

*This is a great all-natural recipe for those wanting to start their day in a healthy, low fat, high fiber way.*

1 1/2 cups oat bran
1/4 cup + 2 tablespoons unprocessed wheat bran
3 tablespoons cinnamon

Combine oat bran, wheat bran and cinnamon; mix well. Put in pint jar and pack. Seal jar. Yield: 17 servings of oatmeal.

Attach the following recipe to the jar:

Low Fat Oatmeal

1/2 cup low fat milk
2 tablespoons mix from jar
2 tablespoons raisins or dried cranberries

Add 2 tablespoons oatmeal from the jar to 1/2 cup low fat milk and stir. Microwave, covered, for 1 minute. Add fruit and let stand 5 minutes to thicken. (optional – add 1/2 teaspoon sugar or Truvia, or 1/2 of a mashed banana) Thin with milk, as desired.

# JAR MIXES

This section is all about spices and seasoning recipes to mix and give away (or keep for yourself!). In this section, the recipient does not need to do anything but cook with jar contents. Many of the seasoning mixes found at craft shows are right here.

# All-Purpose Salt Substitute

FILLS ONE HALF-PINT (8 OZ.) GLASS JAR

This recipe makes 1 cup, which will fit in one half pint (8 oz.) jar or 2 quarter pint jars.

6 tablespoons onion powder
3 tablespoons poultry seasoning
3 tablespoons paprika
2 tablespoons dry mustard
1 tablespoon garlic powder
2 teaspoons ground oregano
2 teaspoons freshly ground black pepper
1 teaspoon chili powder

Mix all ingredients together and place in half pint jar. Seal jar.

Attach the following recipe to the jar:

All-Purpose Salt Substitute

Use this table salt alternative on all your favorite foods.

# Salad Herb Blend – No Salt

## FILLS ONE HALF-PINT (8 OZ.) GLASS JAR

1/4 cup dried parsley
1/4 cup marjoram
2 1/2 tablespoons dried basil
1 1/2 tablespoons sesame seeds
1 1/2 tablespoons chili pepper flakes
1 1/2 tablespoons powdered rosemary
1 1/4 tablespoons powdered celery seed
2 1/2 teaspoons dried savory
2 1/2 teaspoons rubbed sage
2 1/4 teaspoons dried thyme
2 teaspoons onion powder
2 teaspoons dried dill weed
1 1/4 teaspoons finely ground black pepper
1/4 teaspoon garlic powder

In bowl, combine all ingredients. Pour into jar; seal jar. Makes 1 cup.

Attach the following recipe to the jar:

Salad Herb Blend – No Salt

Add herb blend to salad greens before adding dressing. Or sprinkle over pasta salad. Store jar in a cool, dry place.

**\*\*Quantity Recipe for Salad Herb Blend:** *Same recipe increased to fit in 5 half pint (8 oz.) jars or 10 quarter pint jars, for your convenience:*

*1 cup dried parsley*
*1 cup marjoram*
*1/2 cup + 2 tablespoons dried basil*
*1/4 cup + 2 tablespoons sesame seeds*
*1/4 cup + 2 tablespoons chili pepper flakes*
*1/4 cup + 2 tablespoons powdered rosemary*
*1/4 cup powdered celery seed*
*3 tablespoons + 1 teaspoon dried savory*
*3 tablespoons + 1 teaspoon rubbed sage*
*3 tablespoons dried thyme*
*2 tablespoons + 2 teaspoons onion powder*
*2 tablespoons + 2 teaspoons dried dill weed*
*1 tablespoon + 2 teaspoons finely ground black pepper*
*1 teaspoon garlic powder*

# By The Teaspoon Herb Seasoning

## FILLS ONE QUARTER-PINT GLASS JAR

1 teaspoon cayenne pepper
6 teaspoons garlic powder
2 teaspoons dried basil
2 teaspoons dried marjoram
2 teaspoons dried thyme
2 teaspoons dried parsley
2 teaspoons dried savory
2 teaspoons mace
2 teaspoons onion powder
2 teaspoons freshly ground black pepper
2 teaspoons rubbed sage

In bowl, combine all ingredients. Pour into jar; seal jar.

Attach the following recipe to the jar:

By the Teaspoon Herb Seasoning

Use as seasoning in casseroles, stews or fresh vegetable dishes. Use 1 teaspoon or less to taste. Store jar in a cool, dry place.

**Quantity Recipe for By the Teaspoon Herb Seasoning:** *Same recipe increased to fit in 4 half pint (8 oz.) jars or 8 quarter pint (4 oz.) jars, for your convenience:*

*2 teaspoons cayenne pepper*
*1/4 cup garlic powder*
*4 teaspoons dried basil*
*4 teaspoons dried marjoram*
*4 teaspoons dried thyme*
*4 teaspoons dried parsley*
*4 teaspoons dried savory*
*4 teaspoons mace*
*4 teaspoons onion powder*
*4 teaspoons freshly ground black pepper*
*4 teaspoons rubbed sage*

# Low-Salt All-Purpose Seasoning Mix

## FILLS ONE HALF-PINT (8 OZ.) GLASS JAR

*This recipe makes 1 cup, which will fit in one half pint (8 oz.) jar or 2 quarter pint jars.*

1 teaspoon pepper
2 teaspoons garlic powder
4 teaspoons dry mustard
4 teaspoons paprika
2 teaspoons leaf thyme, crumbled
2 teaspoons ground celery seed
8 teaspoons leaf basil, crumbled
2 teaspoons dried parsley flakes
2 teaspoons ground marjoram
2 teaspoons curry powder (optional)
2 teaspoons salt
2 tablespoons + 2 teaspoons onion powder

Mix all ingredients together and place in half pint jar. Seal jar.

Attach the following recipe to the jar:

Low-Salt All-Purpose Seasoning Mix

This delicious low salt seasoning blend is great on everything from vegetables to meats and fish. Try it on all your favorite foods.

# SEASONING MIXES

## Barbecue Dry Rub

### FILLS ONE HALF-PINT GLASS JAR

*This will fit perfectly in a half pint jar. It will be a little less than one cup of dry rub, enough for 5 or 6 times of grilling.*

1/3 cup granulated sugar
1/3 cup brown sugar
2 tablespoons salt
1 tablespoon pepper
1 tablespoon paprika

Mix all ingredients together and place in half-pint jar. Seal jar.

Attach the following recipe to the jar:

Barbecue Dry Rub

Rub on your favorite meat before grilling. Great on country style ribs or pork chops.

Store the remaining dry rub in a cool, dry place sealed in this jar until ready to use.

# Cajun Spice Mix

## FILLS ONE QUARTER PINT GLASS JAR

*If you don't want this mix to be very spicy, leave out the red pepper flakes. Also the salt can be reduced to 1 teaspoon if your recipient is watching their salt intake.*

1 tablespoon + 2 teaspoons paprika
1 tablespoon + 1 teaspoon garlic powder
1 tablespoon salt
2 teaspoons onion powder
2 teaspoons cayenne pepper
2 teaspoons ground black pepper
2 1/2 teaspoons dried thyme
2 1/2 teaspoons dried oregano
1 teaspoon red pepper flakes (optional)

Mix all herbs and seasonings together and place a quarter pint jar. Seal jar.

Attach the following recipe to the jar:

Cajun Spice

Use this Cajun spice mix to season chicken, seafood, steaks or vegetables. Great for Cajun shrimp or mix with mayonnaise for Cajun spiced burgers. Spice up red beans and rice or sprinkle on tater tots or potatoes. Also a great spice for chicken wings and jambalaya. Keep on hand for summer barbeques as a rub for meats and fish. Even popcorn perks up with this lively spice.

**Quantity Recipe for Cajun Spice Mix: *Same recipe increased to fit in 4 half pint (8 oz.) jars or 8 quarter pint jars, for your convenience:*

*3/4 cup + 1 tablespoon + 1 teaspoon paprika*
*2/3 cup garlic powder*
*1/2 cup salt*
*1/3 cup onion powder*
*1/3 cup cayenne pepper*
*1/3 cup ground black pepper*
*1/3 cup + 1 tablespoon + 1 teaspoon dried thyme*
*1/3 cup + 1 tablespoon + 1 teaspoon dried oregano*
*2 tablespoons + 2 teaspoons red pepper flakes (optional)*

# Poultry Seasoning

FILLS FOUR HALF-PINT (8 OZ.) GLASS JARS

1 cup dried, crumbled sage leaves
2 cups dried parsley
1 teaspoon dried onion powder
2 tablespoons salt
1 teaspoon freshly ground pepper
1/2 cup ground rosemary
1/4 cup ground marjoram
1/2 teaspoon ground ginger

Mix all herbs and seasonings together and place in 4 half-pint jars. Seal jars.

 Attach the following recipe to the jar:

Poultry Seasoning

Add 1 tablespoon of the seasoning to 1/2 cup of melted butter for rubbing over chicken or turkey before roasting, or use the same amount directly in a bread stuffing.

# Shake-It-And-Bake-It Mix

## FILLS 5 HALF-PINT (8 OZ.) GLASS JARS

2 cups all-purpose flour
2 cups cornmeal
3 tablespoons ground cumin
4 teaspoons onion powder
4 teaspoons garlic powder
4 teaspoons dried oregano, crushed
2 teaspoons cayenne pepper
2 teaspoons salt
2 teaspoons freshly ground black pepper

Mix all ingredients together and place in 5 half pint jars. Seal jars.

Attach the following recipe to the jar:

Shake-It-And-Bake-It

To season a 3-pound chicken, place 1/2 cup of the mix in a large plastic bag. Cut the chicken into serving pieces and place a few pieces into the bag at a time, shaking to coat. Bake for about one hour at 375 degrees F, turning several times.

# Taco Seasoning Mix

## FILLS ONE HALF-PINT (8 OZ.) GLASS JAR

1/4 cup instant minced onion
2 tablespoons salt
2 tablespoons + 2 teaspoons chili powder
1 tablespoon + 1 teaspoon cornstarch
1 tablespoon + 1 teaspoon crushed dried red pepper flakes
1 tablespoon + 1 teaspoon instant minced garlic
2 teaspoons dried oregano
1 tablespoon + 1 teaspoon ground cumin

Mix all ingredients together and place in half-pint jar. Seal jar.

Attach the following recipe to the jar:

Taco Filling

1 lb. lean ground beef
1/2 cup water
2 tablespoons taco seasoning mix from jar

Brown ground beef in a skillet over medium-high heat. Drain grease. Add water and taco seasoning mix. Simmer on medium for 10 minutes, stirring occasionally. Yield: 8 tacos. Can also be used for enchiladas, shredded chicken or meatloaf.

# Spaghetti Seasoning Mix

## FILLS ONE HALF-PINT (8 OZ.) GLASS JAR

1/4 cup parsley flakes
1/4 cup instant minced onion
1/4 cup cornstarch
2 tablespoons + 2 teaspoons green pepper flakes
2 tablespoons salt
1 tablespoon + 1 teaspoon sugar
1 teaspoon instant minced garlic
1 tablespoon Italian seasoning or combination of Italian herbs (oregano, thyme, sage, basil, marjoram, rosemary)

Mix all ingredients together and place in half pint jar. Seal jar.

Attach the following recipe to the jar:

Spaghetti Sauce

1 lb. lean ground beef
3 cups tomato juice or water
2 (8-oz.) cans tomato sauce
1 (6-oz.) can tomato paste
1/3 cup spaghetti seasoning mix from jar

Brown ground beef in a skillet over medium-high heat. Drain grease. Mix in tomato juice or water, tomato sauce and tomato paste. Stir in 1/3 cup spaghetti seasoning mix from jar. Reduce heat and simmer 30 minutes, stirring occasionally. Spaghetti seasoning mix can also be used in lasagna and pizza sauce. Yield: 4 to 6 servings.

# Sloppy Joe Seasoning

## FILLS ONE HALF-PINT (8 OZ.) GLASS JAR

1/4 cup + 3 tablespoons instant minced onion
2 tablespoons + 1 teaspoon green pepper flakes
2 tablespoons + 1 teaspoon cornstarch
2 tablespoons + 1 teaspoon salt
1 tablespoon + 1/2 teaspoon instant minced garlic
1 3/4 teaspoons celery seed
1 3/4 teaspoons dry mustard
1 3/4 teaspoons chili powder

Mix all ingredients together and place in half-pint jar. Seal jar.

 Attach the following recipe to the jar:

Sloppy Joes

1 lb. lean ground beef
3 tablespoons sloppy joe seasoning mix from jar
1 (8-oz.) can tomato sauce
1/2 cup water
6 hamburger buns

Brown ground beef in a skillet over medium-high heat and drain grease. Add seasoning mix, water and tomato sauce. Bring to a boil. Reduce heat to medium-low and simmer about 10 minutes, stirring occasionally. Serve on hamburger buns. Yield: 6 servings.

# Fajita Seasoning

## FILLS ONE HALF-PINT (8 OZ.) GLASS JAR

1/4 cup and 1 tablespoon cornstarch
3 tablespoons and 1 teaspoon chili powder
1 tablespoon and 2 teaspoons paprika
1 tablespoon and 2 teaspoons salt
1 tablespoon and 2 teaspoons white sugar
2-1/2 teaspoons ground cumin
2-1/2 teaspoons garlic powder
2-1/2 teaspoons onion powder
1 teaspoon cayenne pepper

Mix all ingredients together and place in half-pint jar. Seal jar.

Attach the following recipe to the jar:

Fajitas

1/4 cup water
4 tablespoons fajita seasoning from jar

Mix water and fajita seasoning together and sprinkle over beef or chicken strips while cooking. Add onions and peppers.

# Herbed Cream Cheese Spread

## FILLS ONE QUARTER-PINT GLASS JAR

4 teaspoons dried chives
4 teaspoons caraway seed
4 teaspoons dried dill
4 teaspoons dried basil
2 teaspoons garlic powder
1/2 teaspoon black pepper

Mix all ingredients together and place in quarter pint jar. Seal jar.

 Attach the following recipe to the jar:

Herbed Cream Cheese Spread

1 (8 oz.) package cream cheese, softened
4 1/2 teaspoons of herb mix from jar

Blend herb mix from jar into softened cream cheese. Form into a ball. Keep refrigerated. Serve with assorted crackers or pretzel sticks. This jar mix will make 4 cheese balls.

# Farmhouse Buttermilk Dressing

## FILLS ONE HALF-PINT (8 OZ.) GLASS JAR

1/4 cup + 1 1/2 tablespoons dried parsley
3 tablespoons salt
1 tablespoon + 1 1/2 teaspoons dried chives
1 tablespoon + 1 1/2 teaspoons dried oregano
1 tablespoon + 1 1/2 teaspoons dried tarragon
1 tablespoon + 1 1/2 teaspoons garlic powder
1 tablespoon + 1 1/2 teaspoons pepper
1 tablespoon + 1 1/2 teaspoons dried cilantro

Mix all ingredients together and place in half pint jar. Seal jar.

Attach the following recipe to the jar:

Farmhouse Buttermilk Dressing Mix

1/2 cup mayonnaise
1/2 cup buttermilk
1 tablespoon Buttermilk Dressing Mix from jar

Blend mayonnaise and buttermilk; stir in dressing mix. Refrigerate until ready to use.

# Dry Italian Seasoning Mix

FILLS ONE HALF-PINT GLASS JAR

4 tablespoons dried oregano
3 tablespoons salt
2 tablespoons garlic powder
2 tablespoons dried parsley
2 tablespoons white sugar
2 tablespoons onion powder
2 teaspoons dried basil
2 teaspoons ground black pepper
1 teaspoon black pepper
1/2 teaspoon celery salt
1/2 teaspoon dried thyme

Combine all ingredients and place in half pint jar. Seal jar. Yield: 1 cup.

Attach the following recipe to the jar:

Use jar mix as is in any recipe that calls for Italian seasoning.

Italian Dressing

1/4 cup white vinegar
1/2 to 2/3 cup olive oil or canola oil
2 tablespoons water

Combine vinegar, oil and water in a container with a lid. Add 2 tablespoons of Italian seasoning mix from jar and shake well. Also good as a bread dip.

# Cajun Fry Mix

## FILLS ONE PINT GLASS JAR

1 cup all-purpose flour
2/3 cup corn flour
1/3 cup corn meal
1 tablespoon + 1 teaspoon Old Bay seasoning
1 tablespoon baking powder
1 tablespoon salt
1 tablespoon onion powder
1 tablespoon garlic powder
1/2 teaspoon cayenne pepper

Mix all ingredients together and place in pint jar. Seal jar.

 Attach the following recipe to the jar:

Cajun Fry

Toss your favorite veggies, fish, shellfish, or even cheese in this seasoned mixture to coat before frying. For thicker breading, dip in a mixture of 1 cup milk and 1 beaten egg before rolling in Cajun Fry mix.

# Chili Seasoning Mix

## FILLS ONE QUARTER-PINT GLASS JAR

*If your recipient doesn't like it hot, decrease the red pepper in the recipe below to 1 teaspoon.*

2 tablespoons chili powder
1 tablespoon crushed red pepper
1 tablespoon + 1 teaspoon dried minced onion
1 tablespoon + 1 teaspoon dried minced garlic
3 teaspoons white sugar
3 teaspoons ground cumin
3 teaspoons dried parsley
3 teaspoons salt
1 1/4 teaspoons dried basil
1/4 teaspoon ground black pepper

Mix all ingredients together and place in quarter pint jar. Seal jar.

Attach the following recipe to the jar:

Chili

1 lb. hamburger
2 tablespoons of chili seasoning from jar
1 (14.5 oz.) can diced tomatoes
1 (15 oz.) can tomato sauce
1 can Ranch style beans, drained and rinsed

In a large saucepan, brown hamburger; drain grease. Add 2 tablespoons of seasoning from the jar, tomatoes and tomato sauce and simmer on low for 1/2 hour or longer. Add beans and simmer for 15 to 30 minutes longer. Can also be made in a slow cooker.

# Thousand Island or Ranch Dressing

## FILLS 4 HALF-PINT GLASS JARS

1 1/4 cups dried parsley flakes
5/8 cup onion powder
5/8 cup saltine crackers, finely crushed
5/8 cup garlic powder
5/8 cup dried minced onion
1/3 cup onion salt
1/3 cup garlic salt
2 1/2 tablespoons dill weed

Mix all ingredients together and place in jars. Seal jar.

Attach the following recipe to the jar:

Thousand Island or Ranch Dressing

*To make Ranch Dressing:*
2 cups buttermilk
2 cups mayonnaise
2 tablespoons of mix from jar
Combine all ingredients. Keep refrigerated. Yield: 4 cups.

*To make Thousand Island Dressing:*
2 cups buttermilk
2 cups mayonnaise
1 cup chili sauce
1/2 cup sweet pickle relish
2 tablespoons of mix from jar
Combine all ingredients. Keep refrigerated. Yield 5 1/2 cups.

# Chicken or Beef Gravy Mix

## FILLS TWO HALF-PINT GLASS JARS

1 (2 1/4 oz.) jar instant chicken or beef bouillon granules
1 1/2 cups all-purpose flour
3/4 teaspoon pepper
2 teaspoons onion powder
2 teaspoons garlic powder

 Combine bouillon, flour and pepper. Place in half pint jar. Seal jar.

Attach the following recipe to the jar:

To Make Gravy:

1 1/2 cups water
3 tablespoons margarine or butter

In a saucepan, melt butter or margarine, then add 1/4 cup of gravy mix from jar. Cook and stir until lightly browned, about 1 minute. Whisk in water until smooth. Bring to a boil; cook and stir until thickened, about 2 minutes. Yield: 1 1/2 cups.

# Brown Gravy Mix

## FILLS TWO HALF-PINT GLASS JARS

5 tablespoons beef bouillon granules
1 3/8 cups cornstarch
1 1/3 teaspoons instant coffee crystals
1 1/2 teaspoons onion powder
1 teaspoon garlic powder
1/2 teaspoon paprika
1/2 teaspoon black pepper

Combine all ingredients; mix well. Place in two half-pint jars. Seal jar.

Attach the following recipe to the jar:

To Make Gravy:

1 1/2 cups water
3 tablespoons brown gravy mix from jar

In a saucepan, add water plus 3 tablespoons gravy mix from jar. Bring to a boil; cook and stir until thickened, about 1 minute.

# BREAD DIPPING MIXES

## Tuscan Bread Dipping Mix

### FILLS ONE HALF-PINT GLASS JAR

1/4 cup finely minced garlic
1/4 cup dried rosemary
1/4 cup dried thyme
1/4 cup dried basil
1 teaspoon pepper
1 teaspoon salt

Mix all ingredients together. Using a mortar & pestle, coffee grinder or food processor, grind the mixture until all ingredients are about the same consistency. Place in half pint jar. Seal jar.

 Attach the following recipe to the jar:

Tuscan Bread Dipping Blend

1/4 cup olive oil
1/2 teaspoon sun-dried tomato paste
1 teaspoon mix from jar

In a bowl, pour olive oil and add 1 teaspoon Tuscan Bread Dipping Blend mix from the jar to the oil. Stir the spices into the oil. Add tomato paste in the center of bowl.

# Italian Bread Dipping Blend

## FILLS ONE HALF-PINT GLASS JAR

2 tablespoons black pepper
2 tablespoons dried oregano
2 tablespoons dried rosemary
2 tablespoons dried basil
2 tablespoons dried parsley
2 tablespoons garlic powder
2 tablespoons minced garlic
2 tablespoons crushed red pepper (optional)
2 teaspoons salt

Mix all ingredients together. Using a mortar & pestle, coffee grinder or food processor, grind the mixture until all ingredients are about the same consistency. Place in half pint jar. Seal jar.

Attach the following recipe to the jar:

Italian Bread Dipping Blend

To use, put 1 tablespoon of bread dipping blend on a small plate. Pour 5 to 6 tablespoons extra virgin olive oil over it and blend together. Add fresh Italian bread. Also try adding a little melted butter to the olive oil.

# DIP MIXES

*These recipes that will fit in one half pint (8 oz.) jar can also be halved and placed in 2 quarter pint jars.*

## Bacon-Flavored Dip Mix

### FILLS ONE HALF-PINT GLASS JAR

1/2 cup instant bacon bits
1/4 cup instant minced onion
1 tablespoon + 1 teaspoon instant beef bouillon
1/2 teaspoon instant minced garlic

Mix all ingredients together and place in half pint jar. Seal jar.

Attach the following recipe to the jar:

Bacon-Flavored Dip

*Vary this dip by substituting sour cream with an 8-oz. package softened cream cheese or 1 cup of plain yogurt.*

1 cup sour cream
3 tablespoons dip mix from jar

Combine sour cream and bacon-flavored dip mix. Refrigerate for 1/2 hour before serving. Yield: 1 cup.

# Onion Dip Mix

## FILLS ONE HALF-PINT GLASS JAR

1/4 cup + 1 tablespoon instant minced onion
1/2 cup instant beef bouillon
1 teaspoon +1/4 teaspoon garlic salt

Mix all ingredients together and place in a half pint jar. Seal jar.

Attach the following recipe to the jar:

Onion Dip

1 cup sour cream or 8 oz. package of cream cheese, softened
1 tablespoon grated Parmesan cheese
3 tablespoons onion dip mix from jar

Combine sour cream or cream cheese, Parmesan cheese and onion dip mix from jar. Refrigerate for 1/2 hour before serving. Yield: 1 cup.

# Ranch-Style Seasoning

## FILLS ONE QUARTER-PINT GLASS JAR

2 tablespoons + 2 teaspoons dried parsley
4 teaspoons ground black pepper
4 teaspoons garlic powder
2 teaspoons seasoned salt
2 teaspoons sea salt
2 teaspoons onion powder
1 teaspoon dried thyme
1 teaspoon dill weed

Mix all ingredients together and place in a quarter pint jar. Seal jar.

Attach the following recipe to the jar:

Ranch-Style Seasoning

FOR RANCH DIP: Mix one tablespoon seasoning from jar with 1 3/4 cups sour cream and 1/4 cup of buttermilk.

-OR-

FOR RANCH DIP (Variation): Mix one tablespoon seasoning from jar with 1/4 cup buttermilk, 1 8 oz. container fat-free plain yogurt and 1/2 cup light mayonnaise.

FOR RANCH DRESSING: Mix one tablespoon seasoning from jar with 1 cup mayonnaise and 1 cup buttermilk.

Use one tablespoon of seasoning in place of one package of Ranch dressing mix in recipes.

---

**Quantity Recipe for Ranch-Style Seasoning:** *Same recipe increased to fit in 6 quarter-pint jars, for your convenience:*

1 cup dried parsley
1/2 cup ground black pepper
1/2 cup garlic powder
1/4 cup seasoned salt
1/4 cup sea salt
1/4 cup onion powder
2 tablespoons dried thyme
2 tablespoons dill weed

# Southwest Fiesta Dip Mix

## FILLS ONE PINT GLASS JAR

1/2 cup dried parsley
1/3 cup chili powder
1/3 cup minced onion
1/4 cup salt
1/4 cup ground cumin
1/4 cup dried chives

Mix all ingredients together and place in pint jar. Seal jar.

Attach the following recipe to the jar:

Southwest Fiesta Dip

1 cup sour cream or plain yogurt
1 cup mayonnaise
3 tablespoons fiesta dip mix from jar

Combine dip mix from jar with sour cream or yogurt and mayonnaise. Whisk until smooth. Refrigerate for a few hours before serving. Serve with fresh vegetables, tortilla chips, taquitos, fish tacos, onion rings or fried pickles. Yield: 2 cups.

Southwest Fiesta Dip

1 cup sour cream or plain yogurt
1 cup mayonnaise

Combine 3 tablespoons of
Mexican Fiesta Dip from jar with
sour cream or yogurt and
mayonnaise. Whisk until smooth.
Refrigerate for a few hours before
serving. Serve with fresh
vegetables or tortilla chips.

# Vegetable Dip Mix

## FILLS ONE HALF-PINT GLASS JAR

1/2 cup dried chives
1 tablespoon + 1 teaspoon dill weed
2 tablespoons + 2 teaspoons garlic salt
1 tablespoon + 1 teaspoon paprika

Mix all ingredients together and place in half pint jar. Seal jar.

 Attach the following recipe to the jar:

Vegetable Dip

1 tablespoon lemon juice
1 cup mayonnaise
1 cup sour cream
2 tablespoons vegetable dip mix from jar

Combine all ingredients. Refrigerate for 1/2 hour before serving. Yield: 2 cups.

# Smoked Salmon Spread

## FILLS 4 HALF-PINT GLASS JARS

2 (8 oz.) packages cream cheese, softened
1 teaspoon Worcestershire sauce
1 teaspoon dill weed
3 tablespoons chopped green onion
3 drops hot pepper sauce
12 ounces smoked salmon, chopped

In a medium bowl, combine cream cheese, Worcestershire sauce, dill weed, onion and pepper sauce. Add salmon; mix well. Put into jars, cover and store in refrigerator.

# JAR FILLS

This section is food items to make and fill the jars with. The recipient only has to open and eat!

# JAMS AND SAUCES

The following jams and sauces are not ones that need boiled water bath canning or sterilizing. These are merely foods that can be packed in jars and will last in the refrigerator for a few weeks. The labels include the words "Refrigerate" so your recipient knows they need to be kept cool.

*A little about expiration dates:*

Your jam should last for 3 weeks in the refrigerator. Also look at the best-before or best-by date of the ingredients you are using to make the jam or sauce, and this will give you a clue on how long your jam will last. You may want to write an expiration date on the label of the jam.

# Pumpkin Butter

## FILLS 5 HALF-PINT GLASS JARS

1 (29 oz.) can pumpkin puree
1 1/2 cups granulated sugar
3/4 cup apple juice
2 teaspoons ground cinnamon
2 teaspoons ground ginger
1 teaspoon ground nutmeg
1/2 teaspoon ground cloves

In a large saucepan, combine all ingredients; mix well. Bring mixture to a boil. Reduce heat; simmer for 30 minutes or until thickened, stirring frequently. Pour into half pint jars. Refrigerate.

Add pumpkin butter to yogurt, make a pumpkin and peanut butter sandwich, spread it on waffles, mix it with cream cheese as a spread for bread or graham crackers, even try it with cream in your coffee! Keep refrigerated.

# Banana Jam

## FILLS ONE PINT GLASS JAR

3 cups sliced, ripe bananas
1 1/2 cups granulated sugar
1/4 cup orange juice
3 tablespoons lemon juice
1/4 teaspoon ground nutmeg
1/4 teaspoon cinnamon
2 whole cloves

Combine all ingredients in a deep bowl. Microwave on HIGH until sugar dissolves, 5 to 10 minutes, stirring several times. Continue cooking on HIGH until thickened, about 8 to 12 minutes. Pour into jars and let stand until set. Refrigerate. Yield: 1 pint.

# Pineapple Jam

## FILLS 2 PINT AND 1 HALF-PINT GLASS JARS

1 (20-ounce) can unsweetened, crushed pineapple
3 1/4 cups granulated sugar
1/2 lemon, thinly sliced
3 ounces liquid fruit pectin
1 cup chopped walnuts (optional)

Combine ingredients except nuts and microwave on HIGH for 12 to 15 minutes or until pineapple is no longer crisp. Add walnuts and stir until thickened. Pour into jars, cover and store in refrigerator. Yield: 5 cups.

# Caramel Sauce

## FILLS 2 HALF-PINT GLASS JARS

*Delicious with ice cream, apples and cinnamon rolls. Warm before serving. Keep refrigerated.*

1/3 cup water
1 1/2 cups granulated sugar
2 tablespoons unsalted butter
1 1/4 cups heavy cream
1/2 teaspoon vanilla extract
1/8 teaspoon salt

In a large saucepan, simmer water, sugar and butter over medium heat. Don't stir mixture until the sugar is completely dissolved in the water. Cook uncovered for 5 to 10 minutes, stirring occasionally, until the mixture is golden brown.

Stirring constantly, carefully and gradually pour cream into the mixture. The hot mixture will quickly boil when the cream is added and solidify in spots. Add vanilla extract and salt. Continue stirring over low heat for 5 to 10 minutes until mixture is creamy and smooth. Pour into jars and cool for 1/2 hour. Refrigerate.

# Hot Fudge Sauce

## FILLS 2 HALF-PINT GLASS JARS

1/2 cup cocoa
3/4 cup granulated sugar
2/3 cup milk or water
1/3 cup light corn syrup
1/3 cup butter or margarine
1 teaspoon vanilla

In a medium saucepan, mix cocoa and sugar together. Add milk or water and corn syrup; mix well. Cook over medium heat until mixture boils, stirring constantly. Boil and stir for one minute. Remove pan from heat and mix in butter or margarine and vanilla. Pour into jars, cover and store in refrigerator. Yield: 2 cups.

# Apple Dip

## FILLS 3 HALF-PINT GLASS JARS

1 cup brown sugar
2 (8 oz.) packages cream cheese, softened
2 tablespoons vanilla extract

Mix together brown sugar, cream cheese and vanilla extract until sugar has dissolved and apple dip is smooth. Put in jars, cover and store in refrigerator. Yield: 3 cups.

# SOUP

## Special Cream Soup Mix

### FILLS ONE QUART GLASS JAR

2 cups dry powdered milk
3/4 cup cornstarch
1/4 cup instant chicken bouillon granules (can use low sodium or no sodium)
2 tablespoons onion flakes
1 teaspoon thyme
1 teaspoon basil
1/4 teaspoon Mrs. Dash seasoning or 1/4 teaspoon white pepper

Mix all ingredients together and place in quart jar. Seal jar.

 Attach the following recipe to the jar:

Special Cream Soup

For soup, mix 1/3 cup mix from jar with 1 1/2 cups cold water. Heat over low heat until mixture thickens.

For different flavor soup, add to the above one of the following:

Celery soup – 1/3 cup minced celery
Mushroom soup – 1/4 cup minced or sliced mushrooms
Potato soup – 1 cup diced and cooked potatoes

Chicken soup – 1/4 cup minced cooked chicken
Vegetable soup – 3/4 cup cooked vegetables

Cook over low heat, stirring frequently, until ingredients are tender and soup is hot.

# Chicken Tortilla Soup Mix

## FILLS ONE QUART GLASS JAR

1 cup white or brown long grain rice
3 cups tortilla chips, slightly crushed
1/4 cup dried chopped or minced onion
2 tablespoons chicken bouillon granules
1 teaspoon sugar
1 teaspoon chili powder
1 teaspoon dried cilantro leaves
1 teaspoon lemon pepper
1/2 teaspoon salt
1/2 teaspoon pepper
1/2 teaspoon garlic powder
1/2 teaspoon ground cumin

Add rice to a quart jar. Place the crushed tortilla chips in a small resealable plastic bag. In a small bowl, mix the onion, chicken bouillon, sugar, chili powder, cilantro, lemon pepper, salt, pepper, garlic powder and cumin; place the seasonings in another small resealable plastic bag. Add the 2 plastic bags to the quart jar. Seal jar.

Attach the following recipe to the jar:

Chicken Tortilla Soup

10 cups water
1 (14 1/2 oz.) can Mexican-style stewed tomatoes
1 (4 oz.) can diced green chilies
1 (5 oz.) can chicken, drained
Optional - 1 (15 oz.) can black beans, rinsed and drained

Remove tortilla chips from the jar; set aside. Combine water, tomatoes, rice from jar and seasoning packet from the jar in a Dutch oven or large saucepan. Bring to a boil over high heat; reduce heat, cover and simmer for 20 minutes or until rice is tender.

Add can of chicken to the pot (and optional beans) and heat thoroughly. Sprinkle crushed tortilla chips over each serving. Yield: 3 quarts.

# Chicken Noodle Soup

FILLS ONE PINT GLASS JAR

1 cup fine egg noodles, uncooked
1 1/2 tablespoons chicken bouillon
1/2 teaspoon black pepper
1/4 teaspoon thyme
1/8 teaspoon garlic powder
1/8 teaspoon celery seeds
1 bay leaf

Mix all the spices together with the bouillon and place in a pint jar. Add egg noodles on top. Seal jar.

Attach the following recipe to the jar:

Chicken Noodle Soup

8 cups water
2 stalks celery, diced
2 carrots, diced
1/4 cup minced onion
3 cups cooked, diced chicken

Combine contents of jar and water in a large Dutch oven. Add celery, carrots and onion; bring to a boil. Cover the soup and simmer for 15 minutes. Discard bay leaf. Stir in the chicken and simmer an additional 5 minutes.

# Good Will Soup Mix

FILLS ONE QUART GLASS JAR

1/2 cup dry split peas
1/3 cup beef bouillon granules
2 teaspoons Italian seasoning
1/4 cup pearl barley
1/2 cup dry lentils
1/4 cup dried minced onion
1/2 cup uncooked long-grain rice
1/2 cup alphabet macaroni, or other small macaroni

Mix beef bouillon with Italian seasoning. Put split peas in a quart jar, followed by the beef bouillon mixture. Then add to jar in this order: barley, lentils, onion, rice and macaroni. (The macaroni can be placed in a small resealable plastic bag for convenience of removal.) Seal jar.

Attach the following recipe to the jar:

Good Will Soup

1 lb. lean ground beef
1 (28 oz.) can diced tomatoes, undrained
3 quarts water (12 cups)

Remove macaroni from top of jar; set aside. Brown beef In a Dutch oven; drain. Add tomatoes, water and remaining contents of jar. Bring to a boil. Cover and reduce heat. Simmer for 45 minutes, stirring occasionally. Add macaroni and continue cooking, covered, for 15 minutes or until macaroni, peas and beans are tender.

# Country Bean Soup Mix

## FILLS ONE QUART GLASS JAR

*Be sure to pick through the beans before adding them to the jar, making sure there are no stones or non-bean items mixed in. Just spread out each 1/2 cup of beans on a baking sheet before adding them to the jar to sort through them.*

1/2 cup black-eyed peas
1/2 cup small red beans
1/2 cup black beans
1/2 cup white beans
1/2 cup split peas
1/2 cup pinto beans
1/2 cup lentils
1/4 cup dried parsley flakes
1/4 cup dried minced onion
1 teaspoon dried basil
1 teaspoon garlic powder
3 beef bouillon cubes
2 bay leaves

In a quart jar, layer beans in separate layers or mix beans together and add to jar. Mix parsley flakes, onion, basil and garlic powder together; place in a small resealable plastic bag. Add bouillon cubes (unwrapped) and bay leaves to the plastic bag. Put the bag in the jar; seal jar.

 Attach the following recipe to the jar:

Country Bean Soup

8 cups water
1 (14 oz.) can chopped tomatoes, undrained
Salt and pepper

Remove the spice packet from jar; set aside. Place remaining contents of the jar in a Dutch oven and add water. Be sure beans are covered with water and about 1" over. Bring to a rapid boil and boil for 2 minutes. Remove from heat, cover and let beans sit, covered for one hour. Drain and rinse beans.

Add 8 cups of water, contents of spice packet from jar and chopped tomatoes in juice. Bring to a boil over high heat, then reduce heat and simmer about 2 to 2 1/2 hours until beans are tender. Remove bay leaves and season with salt and pepper.

# Onion Soup Mix

## FILLS ONE HALF-PINT GLASS JAR

3/4 cup dried minced onion
1/3 cup beef bouillon granules
1/4 teaspoon celery salt
1/4 teaspoon granulated sugar
4 teaspoons onion powder

Mix all ingredients together and place in a half-pint jar. Pack and seal jar.

Attach the following recipe to the jar:

Onion Soup:

To Make Onion Soup:

Combine 4 cups water with 5 tablespoons soup mix from the jar. Bring to a boil; simmer, uncovered, for 10 minutes.

To Make Roasted Potatoes:

Toss 5 tablespoons soup mix from the jar with peeled and cubed potatoes and 1/3 cup olive oil. Spoon onto a 10x15-inch baking sheet. Bake at 450 degrees for 35 to 40 minutes, or until potatoes are tender.

To Make Onion Dip:

Blend 5 tablespoons soup mix from the jar with 2 cups sour cream. Stir well and refrigerate at least 2 hours. Stir again before serving with fresh vegetables or potato chips.

# RICE AND STUFFING

## Herbed Rice Mix

### FILLS ONE PINT GLASS JAR

1 1/3 cups long-grain rice
1/4 cup + 2 tablespoons dried celery flakes
2 tablespoons dried minced onion
1 tablespoon + 2 teaspoons dried parsley flakes
1 teaspoon dried chives
1/2 teaspoon dried tarragon
3/4 teaspoon salt
1/2 teaspoon pepper

Mix all ingredients together and place in pint jar. Seal jar.

Attach the following recipe to the jar:

Herbed Rice

2/3 cups water
1 teaspoon butter or margarine

*To prepare 1 serving of rice:*
In a saucepan over medium heat, bring water and butter to a boil. Add 1/4 cup rice mixture from jar. Reduce heat; cover and simmer for 20 minutes. Remove from heat and let stand for about 5 minutes, or until liquid is absorbed. Yield: 8 servings.

# Wild and Crazy Rice Mix

## FILLS 5 PINT GLASS JARS

3 cups wild rice
2 cups golden raisins
1 cup brown rice
1 cup dry lentils
2 cups barley, quick-cooking
3 tablespoons dried parsley flakes
1/4 teaspoon pepper
3 tablespoons instant beef bouillon granules
2 tablespoons dried minced onion
1 tablespoon dried sweet basil
2 teaspoons dried minced garlic
1/2 teaspoon ground allspice

Rinse wild rice, brown rice and lentils and place in a large baking pan. Dry in a 300 degree F oven for about 15 minutes. Stir for even drying. When completely dry, remove from oven and cool. Combine rice and lentils with remaining ingredients. Put in 5 pint glass jars. Seal jars.

Attach the following recipe to the jar:

Wild and Crazy Rice

3 cups water
1 cup sliced mushrooms
1 cup sliced carrots
1/2 cup pecans, toasted & chopped

Combine 1 cup of rice mix from jar with water in a saucepan. Bring to a boil. Cover and reduce heat; simmer 30 minutes. Add mushrooms, carrots and pecans. Simmer 20 to 30 minutes, or until tender. Yield: 6 servings.

# Jambalaya Mix

## FILLS ONE PINT GLASS JAR

1 1/4 cups raw long-grain rice
1 tablespoon parsley
1 tablespoon dried bell pepper flakes
1 bay leaf
2 tablespoons instant minced onion
1 tablespoon Cajun seasoning
2 1/2 teaspoons chicken bouillon granules
1 teaspoon salt
1/2 teaspoon ground black pepper
1/2 teaspoon garlic powder
1/2 teaspoon red pepper flakes

Combine all ingredients except rice and bay leaf. Put rice in a pint jar; add the combined spices on top of rice. Lay bay leaf on top. Seal jar.

Attach the following recipe to the jar:

Jambalaya

3 cups water
1 (16 oz.) can crushed Italian tomatoes
10 oz. Andouille sausage, sliced
1/2 cup cooked shrimp

In a large saucepan, bring water to a boil. Add contents of jar and Italian tomatoes to saucepan. Reduce heat to simmer; add sausage and cook for 20 minutes or until rice is tender. Add shrimp and cook 5 minutes more. Remove and discard bay leaf. Yield: 8 cups.

# Instant Stuffing Mix

## FILLS ONE QUART GLASS JAR

3 1/2 cups unseasoned, toasted bread cubes
3 tablespoons dried celery flakes
1 tablespoon dried parsley
2 teaspoons chicken bouillon granules
2 teaspoons dried minced onion
1/4 teaspoon rubbed sage
1/4 teaspoon poultry seasoning

Place bread cubes in a quart jar. In a small bowl, combine celery flakes, parsley, bouillon, minced onion, sage and poultry seasoning; mix well. Put seasonings in a small resealable plastic bag. Add seasonings bag on top of bread cubes. Seal jar.

Attach the following recipe to the jar:

Instant Stuffing

1 cup water
2 tablespoons butter or margarine

In a saucepan, bring water, butter or margarine and contents of seasoning packet from the jar to a boil. Reduce heat; cover and simmer for 10 minutes. Remove from heat; add bread cubes from the jar and mix gently. Cover and let stand 5 minutes. Toss with a fork before serving. Yield: 6 servings.

# Pizza Crust

FILLS ONE QUART GLASS JAR

2 3/4 cups bread flour
1 package active dry yeast (1 tablespoon)
2 teaspoons salt

Mix all ingredients together and place in a quart jar. Seal jar.

Attach the following recipe to the jar:

Pizza Crust

(Makes 2 (12") pizzas)

2 tablespoons olive oil
1 cup warm water
1 cup tomato sauce
1/2 cup grated Mozzarella cheese
1/3 cup grated Parmesan cheese
1 teaspoon oregano

Place pizza dough mix from the jar in a large bowl; add oil and water. Beat with a spoon until mixture shapes into a ball. Knead on a floured surface for 5 minutes. Transfer to a greased bowl and let the dough rise for 90 minutes for thin crust; 2 hours to 2 hours 15 minutes for thicker crust. Divide dough in half and pat into 2 12-inch circles. Place on baking sheets or pizza baking pans.

Top pizza dough with tomato sauce, oregano and cheeses. Bake at 425 degrees in a preheated oven for 20 to 25 minutes. Let stand 5 minutes before cutting.

# Pancake Mix

## FILLS ONE PINT GLASS JAR

2 cups all-purpose flour
4 tablespoons granulated sugar
5 teaspoons baking powder
1 teaspoon salt

Combine all ingredients and place in a pint jar. Seal jar.

Attach the following recipe to the jar:

Pancake Mix

2 eggs
1/2 cup vegetable oil
2 cups milk

In a large bowl, pour pancake mix from jar; add eggs, oil and milk. Stir until well mixed.

Spray a large skillet or griddle with non-stick cooking spray. Heat griddle over medium heat. Pour 1/4 cup batter onto the griddle. Cook until bubbles form on the surface, then turn over with a spatula and cook to a golden brown color.

These pancakes freeze well after they are cooked. Place each pancake separately in a small resealable plastic bag and place all the small bags in a large freezer-safe resealable plastic bag. Reheat in microwave oven.

# DRINKS

## Bavarian Mint Coffee

FILLS ONE HALF-PINT GLASS JAR

1/3 cup granulated sugar
1/4 cup instant nonfat powdered dry milk
1/4 cup instant coffee
2 tablespoons unsweetened cocoa powder
2 hard peppermint candies, crushed

Mix all ingredients together. In a blender or a food processor, grind the mixture until all ingredients are about the same consistency. Place in a half-pint jar. Seal jar.

Attach the following recipe to the jar:

Bavarian Mint Coffee
In a cup, combine 2 tablespoons of the Bavarian Mint Coffee mix with 2/3 cup of boiling water.

# Vanilla Hot Chocolate

## FILLS ONE HALF-PINT GLASS JAR

2 teaspoons pure vanilla powder
2 teaspoons dried orange peel
1 cup white chocolate chips

In a small bowl, combine all ingredients. Place in a half-pint jar. Seal jar.

 Attach the following recipe to the jar:

Vanilla Hot Chocolate

1 1/2 cups milk
1/4 cup vanilla hot chocolate mix from jar

Heat milk in a small saucepan until almost boiling. Add hot chocolate mix and stir until chocolate is melted. Continue to stir over low heat until hot. Yield: 4 servings.

# Candy Cane Hot Chocolate Mix

## FILLS ONE QUART GLASS JAR

1 1/2 cups confectioners' sugar
1 cup + 2 tablespoons cocoa
1 1/2 cups nondairy creamer
4 4-inch peppermint sticks, crushed
Mini marshmallows

Blend together nondairy creamer and peppermint sticks. In a quart jar, layer ingredients in this order: confectioners' sugar, cocoa, and creamer mixture, packing each layer well. Fill remaining space in top of jar with a layer of mini marshmallows that have been put in a small resealable plastic bag. Seal jar.

Attach the following recipe to the jar:

Candy Cane Hot Chocolate

Remove marshmallows from jar and set aside. Pour the remaining ingredients from the jar into a large mixing bowl; mix well. Spoon the hot chocolate mixture back into canning jar.

In a cup, add 1/4 cup cocoa mixture to 3/4 cup of boiling water; add marshmallows and stir to blend.

# NUTS & SNACKS

## Sugary Cinnamon Pretzels

### FILLS 4 QUART GLASS JARS

*This coating remains stuck to the pretzels surprisingly well. This will fit in 4 quart jars. Or if you need to pack in 5 jars, use the pint and a half jars (found at Wal-Mart). They are as tall as the quart jars but not as wide and hold a little less.*

1 (1 lb.) bag tiny twists pretzels
3/4 cup granulated sugar
3/4 cup vegetable oil
3 teaspoons cinnamon

Line 2 baking sheets with foil. Layer half the pretzels on each baking sheet. In a bowl, combine sugar, oil and cinnamon. Pour the mixture on pretzels, stirring to coat. Bake at 300 degrees F for 25 minutes, stirring once while baking. Allow pretzels to completely cool before packing in 4 quart jars.

# Brownie Brickle Bits

## FILLS 2 TO 3 QUART GLASS JARS

*The secret to making crunchy flat brownie pieces with this recipe is to use a 17" x 11" baking sheet or other large baking sheet. Also non-stick cooking spray with flour works the best so the thin brownies don't stick to the pan.*

1/2 cup butter or margarine
1 ounce unsweetened chocolate
1/2 cup granulated sugar
1 egg
1/4 teaspoon vanilla
1/3 cup all-purpose flour
1/2 cup dark chocolate chips
Non-stick cooking or baking spray

Preheat oven to 375 degrees F. In a large saucepan, melt butter. Remove from heat and add unsweetened chocolate. Stir until chocolate is melted.

Stir in sugar, egg and vanilla. Add flour and mix well. Lightly coat a 17" x 11" baking sheet with cooking spray. Pour batter on the baking sheet and spread as evenly as possible. Sprinkle chocolate chips on top.

Bake for exactly 10 minutes. Cool for 15 minutes, then break brownie brickle into uneven bits and pieces, much like peanut brittle. Fill jars.

Brownie
Brittle

# Chocolate Caramel Pretzels

## FILLS ONE PINT GLASS JAR

15 small square pretzels
15 Hershey's Kisses with Caramel
15 M&M's

Layer M&M's, then pretzels and wrapped Hershey's kisses in the jar. Seal jar.

Attach the following recipe to the jar:

Chocolate Caramel Pretzels

Preheat oven to 275 degrees F. Line a baking sheet with foil. Place pretzels on the foil and center an unwrapped Hershey's Kiss in the center of each pretzel. Bake for 2 minutes at 275 degrees F. Immediately press an M&M in the center of each kiss, pressing down gently so the chocolate kiss spreads out. Refrigerate for 15 minutes until chocolate hardens, then store at room temperature.

# Firecrackers

## FILLS ONE QUART GLASS JAR

40 saltine crackers
2 teaspoons of your favorite grilling spice
Crushed red pepper flakes
1 (10-ounce) brick Cracker Barrel Extra-sharp Cheddar cheese, shredded

Preheat oven to 475 degrees F. Arrange crackers in a single layer, sides touching, in a 10x15-inch cake pan. Sprinkle with grilling spice, then with as many pepper flakes as you dare. Layer cheese evenly over the crackers.

Place pan on the center shelf of the oven. Close oven door and turn off the oven. Leave in the oven for 4 hours. The heated oven will melt and brown the cheese, creating an even coating of crispy brown. Remove from oven and let cool. Break apart and place in a quart jar.

# Spicy Saltines

## FILLS 4 QUART GLASS JARS

1 (16 ounce) box saltine crackers
1 (1 ounce) package ranch dressing mix
1 1/2 cups canola oil
2 tablespoons red pepper flakes
1 tablespoon chili powder
2 - 1 gallon resealable plastic bags

In a bowl, combine ranch dressing mix, oil, red pepper and chili powder. Add half of the crackers to each plastic bag and pour half the oil mixture over them. Seal the bags filled with air. Toss crackers in the bag every 5 minutes for an hour. Let crackers rest overnight or at least for 4 hours before placing them in 4 quart jars. One tube of crackers fits in a quart jar.

# Sugar Coated Pecans

## FILLS 2 PINT GLASS JARS

2 egg whites
1 tablespoon water
1 teaspoon of vanilla
1 pound pecan halves (3 3/4 cups)
3/4 teaspoon salt
1 cup granulated sugar
1 teaspoon ground cinnamon

In a medium bowl, whip egg whites and water together until foamy. Add vanilla. In a separate bowl, mix salt, sugar and cinnamon together.

Add pecans to egg white mix and stir to coat pecans. Lift pecans out of egg white mix with a slotted spoon and mix them in the sugar mixture until well covered. (Or put sugar mixture in a large Ziploc bag, then add nuts to coat.) Lay nuts out on a greased or parchment paper covered baking sheet. Bake at 250 degrees F for 1 hour, stirring every 15 minutes.

# Chocolate Covered Raisins

### FILLS 2 PINT GLASS JARS

1 cup semi-sweet chocolate chips
1/4 cup dark corn syrup
2 cups raisins
2 tablespoons confectioners sugar
1 1/2 teaspoons vanilla extract

Mix together chocolate chips and corn syrup in top of a double boiler; bring water to a boil. Lower heat and cook on low until chocolate chips melt, stirring constantly. Remove from heat, and stir in raisins, confectioners sugar and vanilla. Drop by small spoonfuls on waxed paper. Store in refrigerator. Place in jars. Makes about 5-1/2 dozen.

# Spiced Pretzels

## FILLS 6 QUART GLASS JARS

2 (1 lb.) bags hard pretzels
1 cup canola oil
1 teaspoon garlic salt
1 teaspoon lemon pepper
1 teaspoon dill – or – 1 teaspoon ground cayenne pepper
1 package Ranch dressing

Break pretzels in a shallow pan. Mix oil, spices and ranch dressing. Pour over broken pretzels. Bake at 200 degrees for 45 minutes, stirring once halfway through baking. When cool, pack in 6 quart jars.

# Roasted Chickpea Snack

## FILLS ONE PINT GLASS JAR

1 (15 oz.) can chickpeas

2 tablespoons olive oil

1 tablespoon ground cumin

1 teaspoon garlic powder

1/2 teaspoon chili powder

1/8 teaspoon crushed red pepper

1/8 teaspoon ground black pepper

1/8 teaspoon sea salt

Preheat oven to 350 degrees F. Drain and rinse chickpeas. In a bowl, combine olive oil, ground cumin, garlic powder, chili powder, crushed red pepper, black pepper and sea salt; whisk until well mixed.

Add chickpeas and stir until well coated. Layer chickpeas on a baking sheet. Bake at 350 degrees F for 45 minutes, stirring occasionally, until slightly crispy and nicely browned.

# Spiced Pumpkin Seeds

## FILLS ONE PINT GLASS JAR

1 1/2 tablespoons margarine, melted or olive oil
1/2 teaspoon seasoned salt
1/2 teaspoon salt
1/4 teaspoon garlic powder
2 teaspoons Worcestershire sauce
2 cups whole raw pumpkin seeds

Combine olive oil or margarine, salt, seasoned salt, garlic powder and Worcestershire sauce. Boil the seeds in water for about 35 minutes. Pat dry and combine them with margarine mixture. Mix thoroughly and place in in a single layer on one or two baking sheets. Bake at 300 degrees F for 1 hour, stirring occasionally.

# Granola Skagit

FILLS 2 QUART GLASS JARS OR 4 PINT JARS

4 cups quick cooking oats
1 cup chopped nuts
1 cup wheat germ
1 cup shredded coconut, cut up, or use flaked coconut
1/3 cup melted margarine
1/3 cup honey

In a bowl, combine oats, nuts, wheat germ and coconut together. Combine margarine and honey together, add to oats mixture; mix well. Spread on baking sheets. Bake at 300 degrees F. for 15 minutes. Stir every 5 minutes.

Add:

1 cup diced prunes
1 cup chopped dates

Roll in confectioners' sugar before adding to granola so they don't stick together. Store in sealed jars. Use within a few weeks. Yield: 8 cups.

Exclusively for *100 MORE Easy Recipes In Jars* readers:

# Over 2000 Online Labels and Recipe Cards Available for these recipes at

## www.NorthPoleChristmas.com/jarsbook2.html

Visit http://www.NorthPoleChristmas.com

for Free Christmas Craft Patterns

and Christmas Printables.

# Desserts in Jars

## Bake and No-Bake Recipes

## Bonnie Scott

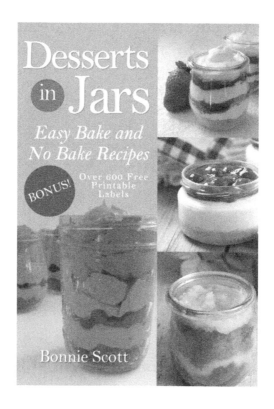

# Desserts in Jars

Desserts in Jars is the latest book in the collection of fun and easy, sure-to-please gift ideas from your kitchen. No matter what the occasion, a dessert is a welcome gift, and jars are the latest trend in home décor and food. Combine the two, and you've made a sure-fire dessert that will be a welcome addition to any gathering or event.

Cakes, puddings, parfaits and more yummy desserts are all made, stored and served in cute, retro-style Mason jars. These stylish serving dishes make perfect containers for any casual get together. Plus, they're sturdy and inexpensive, so you can make up a few or enough to serve the whole clan.

You can add colorful, personalized labels, and these jar desserts are perfect for sending home with your guests at the end of the evening for a late night snack, compliments of you! Small desserts are the perfect way to say "thank you" to teachers, your postman or neighbors. It's also an easy way to send the kids off to school with a lunchtime treat or to pack in your own lunch bag.

Desserts in Jars just may become your go-to gift for all those hard-to-buy-for friends and acquaintances. They're perfect for singles and small families, and a welcome small sweet treat for those who wouldn't appreciate a zillion calorie, full size cake. These single servings are just right to serve at a gathering or potluck, so everyone will get to enjoy your tasty contribution. They're much easier and safer to pack up to take on the road, and you'll never have an emergency stop dessert disaster in your car!

# Tips for Baking in Jars

These recipes are all made with wide mouth half-pint jars canning or mason jars. The shape of the jars is varied in these recipes but the baking time usually was the same, no matter the jar shape.

Make sure the inside of the jar stays clean as you fill it with your ingredients. Wipe the inside (and outside if needed) as you contribute to the jar before baking if there is a mess on the glass.

When layering a non-bake dessert or layering a cake after baking, think about how you will position your layers. A variety in color, texture and thickness adds to the decorative look of your jar.

Baking in jars – please note that the baking time may vary somewhat depending on the shape of jar you are using and your oven, so watch the first go-round of your cake in a jar carefully. You may want to bake just one jar first as a test run to be sure you have the right time and temperature.

Be sure to grease the jars well if you will be baking in them. Non-stick cooking spray works the best, although any method of greasing will work.

-   Use a baking sheet to place the jars on and be sure the jars don't touch. The jars themselves will be very hot since they are glass so handle with care like any other glass baking dish.

-   After the cakes cool, these little jars are a great way to freeze a dessert.

-   Some of the jars used in this book are Weck brand

jars from Germany, like the jar in the photo of Whipped Chocolate Delight. They can be found at World Market. The remainder are canning jars that are available at supermarkets and hobby stores.

- The first recipe – S'mores in a Jar – has step by step photos of how to make a cake (or brownies in this case) in a jar.

# Jar Labels

USE THE LABELS available at

## www.InJars.com/DessertsInJars.html

There is at least 1 page of labels specifically for each recipe in separate pdf files available to print. They can be printed on paper, 2 1/2" white round labels or 2 1/2" round Kraft Brown labels.

The Kraft Brown labels (by Avery) produce a more subdued look to the label because the colors on top of brown won't be as vibrant as the white labels. Use the following Avery labels for these templates:

Avery Kraft Brown 2 1/2" labels #22818

Avery Glossy White 2 1/2" labels #41462

If you don't want to use labels, printing the jar labels on good quality paper works just as well. Cut them out and stick the labels to your jars with double-faced tape.

The labels are available on the web and can be printed at www.InJars.com/DessertsInJars.html.

# DESSERTS TO BAKE

## S'mores in a Jar

Since brownies cook quickly, carefully watch the first batch of brownies so they don't cook too long and dry out. Or, bake a test run with just one jar to see when the brownies are ready – all ovens are different and using a different shape of glass jar than I did can even change the baking time a little.

Brownies:

1/2 cup and 2 tablespoons all-purpose flour
1/2 teaspoon baking powder
1/2 teaspoon salt
1/3 cup unsweetened cocoa powder
1 cup and 2 tablespoons granulated sugar
6 tablespoons butter or margarine, softened
2 eggs, slightly beaten

Topping:

2 graham crackers
3 (1.5 oz.) milk chocolate bars
1 1/4 cups miniature marshmallows

Crush graham crackers into crumbs and put in a small bowl. Break each chocolate bar into about 16 pieces and place in another small bowl. In a final bowl, add marshmallows. Set aside.

In a large bowl, combine flour, baking powder and salt. Mix in cocoa powder and sugar. Add eggs and butter; mix until blended well.

Grease insides of each jar well with butter or spray inside with spray butter. Fill each jar about 1/4 full with about 2 heaping teaspoons of batter; spread batter as evenly as you can in the glass jar.

Place filled jars on a baking sheet, not touching each other. Bake in a preheated oven at 350 degrees F for 15 to 20 minutes. Remove, sprinkle about a teaspoon of crushed graham crackers on top of each brownie, then add 7 pieces of chocolate on top of the graham crackers, followed by about 15 mini-marshmallows. Bake for an additional 5 minutes.

Yield: 7 8-oz. glass jars.

# S'mores in a Jar:

Step 1 – Grease the insides of the jars.

Step 2 – Fill each jar about 1/4 full with batter.

# Root Beer Floats in Jars

1 cup granulated sugar
1/2 cup margarine or butter
2 eggs
2 teaspoons root beer concentrate
2 cups all-purpose flour
1 tablespoon baking powder
1 teaspoon salt
2/3 cup root beer

In a medium bowl, cream sugar and margarine or butter until fluffy and light. Add root beer concentrate and eggs; beat until well mixed. In another bowl, mix together flour, baking powder and salt. Add flour mixture to root beer mixture. Beat in 2/3 cup of root beer just until combined.

Spray jars with non-stick cooking spray. Fill each jar 1/4 to 1/3 full of batter. Place filled jars on a baking sheet, not touching each other. Bake in preheated oven at 375 degrees F for 16 to 18 minutes or until inserted toothpick comes out clean.

### *Assembly*:

Remove jars from oven. Let cool for 10 minutes. Make Root Beer Frosting and Root Beer glaze.

Using a large spoon, scoop out the top half of the cake in each jar (in one piece, if possible). Set aside.

Spoon a heaping tablespoon of *Root Beer Frosting* into each jar, covering the cake. Replace the top half of the cake into the jar.

Top jar off with the remaining frosting.

*To Serve*: Add a scoop of vanilla ice cream on top. Drizzle ice cream with root beer glaze.

Yield: 12 8-oz. glass jars.

*Root Beer Frosting:*

1/2 cup butter or margarine
1/8 cup semi-sweet chocolate chips
1 teaspoon root beer extract
1/4 cup root beer
1/4 cup unsweetened cocoa
2 cups confectioners' sugar

In a small bowl, partially melt butter or margarine and chocolate chips together in microwave, about 20 seconds. Stir until butter or margarine is melted. Add root beer extract, root beer and cocoa; stir until well mixed. Gradually add confectioners' sugar.

*Root Beer Glaze:*

1 cup confectioners' sugar
1/2 teaspoon root beer concentrate
1/4 cup of milk

Combine sugar, root beer concentrate and milk to make glaze.

# Caramel Apple Cakes

*Bake these in the 8 oz. short and wide jars so they resemble caramel apples when finished.*

2 cups all-purpose flour
1 1/4 teaspoons salt
1/2 teaspoon baking powder
1 1/2 teaspoons ground cinnamon + 1/2 teaspoon ground cinnamon
3/4 cup butter + 1/4 cup butter
1 1/3 cups brown sugar, packed + 2/3 cup brown sugar, packed
2 eggs
1/2 teaspoon vanilla
3/4 cup milk
1 cup pecan pieces + 1/4 cup pecans for garnish
2 apples - peeled, cored and chopped into small pieces

In a bowl, combine flour, salt, baking powder and 1 1/2 teaspoons ground cinnamon.

In another bowl, beat 3/4 cup butter and 1 1/3 cups brown sugar until smooth and fluffy. Add eggs and mix well. Stir in vanilla and milk. Add flour mixture and mix just until combined. Fold in 1/2 cup pecan pieces and 1/2 of the apple pieces.

Spray jars with non-stick cooking spray. Fill each jar 1/2 full of batter.

In a saucepan, melt 1/4 cup butter; add 2/3 cup brown sugar and 1/2 teaspoon cinnamon. Bring to a boil, stirring constantly. Spoon mixture on top of batter in each jar. Add 1/2 cup pecans and remaining apple pieces on top.

Place filled jars on a baking sheet, not touching each other. Bake in a preheated oven at 375 degrees F for 50 minutes or until an inserted toothpick comes out clean.

After removing from oven, make *Caramel Frosting*. Let jars cool for about 10 minutes, then put a heaping tablespoon of frosting on top of the hot cake in each jar. Add a few nuts as garnish. Add a popsicle stick in the center of each cake for a caramel apple look.

Yield: 10 8-oz. wide-mouth jars.


*Caramel Frosting:*

3/4 cup brown sugar, packed
1/3 cup half-and-half cream
1/4 cup butter, melted
1/2 teaspoon vanilla extract
1 3/4 cups confectioners' sugar

In a medium saucepan, combine brown sugar, cream and butter. Bring to a boil, stirring frequently. Remove from heat and stir in vanilla and confectioners' sugar. Beat with an electric mixer until fluffy, about 5 minutes.

Yield: 1 1/2 cups.

# Chocolate Pudding Cakes

3/4 cup all-purpose flour
1/2 cup cocoa powder
1/2 cup granulated sugar
1 1/2 teaspoons baking powder
1/2 teaspoon salt
1/2 cup milk or soy milk
3 tablespoons applesauce or vegetable oil
1/2 cup brown sugar, packed
1/4 cup miniature semisweet chocolate chips
2 teaspoons vanilla extract
1 1/4 cups half & half

Spray jars with non-stick cooking spray. In a bowl, combine flour, 1/4 cup of cocoa powder, granulated sugar, baking powder and salt. Mix in milk and applesauce or oil. Divide mixture evenly into 6 8-oz. glass jars.

Mix together brown sugar, 1/4 cup of cocoa powder and chocolate chips. Add on top of mixture in jars, dividing evenly between jars.

Heat half & half in microwave until very hot but not boiling. Add vanilla to the half & half, then pour on top of mixture in each jar, distributing evenly (between 3 and 4 tablespoons per jar). Do not stir.

Place filled jars on a baking sheet, not touching each other. Bake in a preheated oven at 350 degrees F for 30 minutes or until sauce is bubbly. Serve warm or at room temperature. Adding whipped cream or ice cream is optional.

Yield: 6 8-oz. glass jars.

# Fruit Cocktail Cakes

2 cups all-purpose flour
1 1/2 cups granulated sugar
2 teaspoons baking soda
1/4 teaspoon salt
1 can fruit cocktail, 17 oz. (do not drain juice)
2 eggs, beaten
1/2 cup brown sugar
1/2 cup walnuts, chopped

In a bowl, combine flour, sugar, baking soda and salt. Pour fruit cocktail with juice in the bowl. Add eggs. Mix well.

Spray jars with non-stick cooking spray. Fill each jar 1/4 to 1/3 full of batter. Sprinkle top of batter in each jar with brown sugar and walnuts. Place filled jars on a baking sheet, not touching each other. Bake in a preheated oven at 350 degrees F for 20 to 25 minutes.

*Assembly:*
Remove jars from oven. Let cool for 10 minutes. After removing jars from oven, make *Coconut Frosting*.

Using a large spoon, scoop out the top half of the cake in each jar (in one piece, if possible). Set aside.

Spoon heaping tablespoon of hot *Coconut Frosting* into each jar, covering cake. Replace top half of the cake into the jar. Top jar off with the remaining frosting.
Yield: 12 8-oz. glass jars.

*Coconut Frosting:*

1 1/2 cups margarine
1 1/2 cups granulated sugar
1 1/2 cups evaporated milk
2 teaspoons vanilla
2 cups shredded coconut

Combine margarine, sugar and milk in a pan. Cook and after it has started to boil, stir constantly. Boil for 15 to 20 minutes on medium heat, stirring occasionally, until frosting starts getting fairly thick. Take off stove and mix in vanilla; then add coconut.

# Easy Brownies

3/4 cup all-purpose flour
1/2 teaspoon baking powder
1/2 teaspoon salt
1/2 cup cocoa
1 1/2 cups granulated sugar
3/4 cup butter, melted
1 1/2 teaspoons vanilla
3 eggs

Mix together flour, baking powder and salt in a bowl. Add cocoa and sugar. In another bowl, blend melted butter and vanilla. Add eggs and beat well with a spoon. Gradually add dry ingredients to egg mixture and stir until blended well.

Spray jars with non-stick cooking spray. Fill each jar 1/3 full of batter. Place the filled jars on a baking sheet, not touching each other. Bake in preheated oven at 350 degrees F for 20 minutes or until inserted toothpick comes out clean.

Yield: 12 8-oz. glass jars.

# Birthday Cake in a Jar

Yes, you CAN use a store-bought mix for cake in a jar. Let's use this recipe as an example.

This recipe will fill 16 to 20 jars up to the very top with cake if you fill them halfway full with batter. Pile the frosting high if you don't need to add a lid, otherwise remove some cake if needed so the jars can be frosted and closed.

1 box of chocolate cake mix

1.  Spray the jars with non-stick cooking spray.
2.  Follow the directions on the box for mixing the batter.
3.  Fill each jar about half full (or a little less). I used a 1/3 cup measuring cup to pour the batter into the jars.
4.  Wipe any excess batter off the glass and rim of jar.
5.  Put all the jars on one or two baking sheets not touching each other and bake following the instructions for cupcakes on the box, which is about 1/2 the time for cakes. The jars may need 5 minutes more than cupcakes. Use the wooden toothpick test to see if they are done.
6.  Make frosting from recipe below. Divide the finished frosting into 2 bowls and add food coloring to each.
7.  If you want to add frosting to the center of the jar, wait until the jars are cool enough to handle, then scoop out half the cake, add frosting and sprinkles if

you want, then replace the cake and add more frosting on top. Don't forget the candles!

Yield: 16 to 20 8-oz. glass jars.

*Buttercream Frosting:*

1 1/2 cups butter, softened
1 (16 oz.) package confectioners' sugar
2 tablespoons milk
1 teaspoon vanilla extract
Food coloring – 1 or 2 colors

With an electric mixer, beat butter at medium speed until creamy; gradually add sugar, creaming until fluffy and light. Add milk and vanilla, beating to desired consistency. Divide the frosting into 2 small bowls and add food coloring.

Yield: about 4 cups.

# Lemon Cakes

*To make a filled lemon cake in a jar, add a spoonful of vanilla pudding in the middle of each cake before frosting them.*

2 cups all-purpose flour
2 teaspoons baking powder
1/4 teaspoon salt
1 1/3 cups granulated sugar
2/3 cup unsalted butter
3 eggs
3/4 teaspoon vanilla extract
2 tablespoons lemon zest
2/3 cup whole milk, divided
2 tablespoons fresh lemon juice, divided

In a bowl, combine flour, baking powder and salt. In another bowl, with an electric mixer, cream the sugar and butter until fluffy and light. Beat in eggs, one at a time. Mix in lemon zest and vanilla extract.

Add half the flour mixture to the sugar mixture and beat just until combined. Add half the milk and half of the lemon juice and beat. Beat in the remaining half of the flour mixture, then the remaining half of the milk and lemon juice, just until well combined.

Spray jars with non-stick cooking spray. Fill each jar 1/3 full of batter. Place the filled jars on a baking sheet, not touching each other. Bake in preheated oven at 375 degrees F for 17 minutes or until a toothpick inserted in the center comes out clean. While cakes are baking, make *Vanilla Pudding Filling.*

*Assembly*:

Remove jars from oven. Let cool for 10 minutes. After removing jars from oven, make *Lemon Frosting.*

Using a large spoon, scoop out the top half of the cake in each jar (in one piece, if possible). Set aside.

Add *Vanilla Pudding Filling* to the jars, covering the cake. Replace the top half of the cake into the jar.

Top the jar off with *Lemon Frosting*.

Keep refrigerated.

Yield: 12 8-oz. glass jars.

*Vanilla Pudding Filling:*

1/3 cup granulated sugar
3 tablespoons cornstarch
1/4 teaspoon salt
2 cups cold milk
1 tablespoon butter
1 teaspoon vanilla extract

In a medium saucepan, mix together sugar, cornstarch and salt. Add milk, whisk until dissolved. Cook on medium-high heat, stirring constantly, until mixture partially thickens and will cover the back of a metal spoon. (Don't let it boil.) Remove from heat, mix in butter and vanilla. Refrigerate.

*Lemon Frosting:*

1 1/3 cups heavy cream
1/2 cup confectioners' sugar
1 tablespoon fresh lemon juice

With an electric mixer set on low, beat the cream in a chilled bowl until it begins to thicken. Add the confectioners' sugar and lemon juice, a little at a time, beating after each addition. With the mixer on high, beat about 5 minutes or until the frosting forms soft peaks. Yield: 3 cups.

# Spice Muffins in a Jar

3 1/2 cups all-purpose flour
1/4 cup granulated sugar
2 tablespoons baking powder
1 teaspoon baking soda
2 teaspoons ground cinnamon
1 teaspoon ground nutmeg
1/2 teaspoon ground ginger
1/2 teaspoon ground cloves
1 teaspoon salt
1/2 cup butter or margarine, melted
2 eggs
2 teaspoons vanilla
2 cups milk

In a bowl, combine flour, sugar, baking powder, baking soda, cinnamon, nutmeg, ginger, cloves and salt. In another bowl, mix butter, eggs, vanilla and milk; add to dry ingredients and mix well. Batter will be lumpy.

Spray jars with non-stick cooking spray. Fill each jar 1/4 to 1/3 full of batter. Place the filled jars on a baking sheet, not touching each other. Bake in a preheated oven at 400 degrees F for 15 minutes or until inserted toothpick comes out clean. Frost with *Cream Cheese Frosting* and sprinkle frosted jars lightly with cinnamon.

Yield: 12 8-oz. glass jars.

EASY DESSERTS AND RECIPES IN JARS – 3 BOOKS IN 1

*Cream Cheese Frosting:*

1/2 cup butter or margarine, softened
1 (8 oz.) package cream cheese, softened
1 (16 oz.) package confectioners' sugar
1 teaspoon ground cinnamon
1 teaspoon vanilla extract

In a medium bowl, mix together butter or margarine and cream cheese; beat until smooth. Add sugar, cinnamon and vanilla; beat until fluffy and light.

Yield: 3 cups.

# Pulitzer Pudding Cakes

This simple recipe is delicious! And it is so easy to make. This recipe would be excellent for baby showers and other large gatherings. To bake in quantity, make 24 jars using one can of blueberry pie filling, one of cherry and one of apple.

1 can fruit pie filling (any flavor)
1 1/2 cups of a box cake mix
1 cup nuts, chopped
1/2 cup butter

Spray jars with non-stick cooking spray. Divide fruit pie filling evenly between jars. Sprinkle the dry cake mix evenly over the pie filling. Gently shake jars sideways to level out the cake mix. Sprinkle with nuts. Dot with small pieces of butter. Place the filled jars on a baking sheet, not touching each other. Bake in a preheated oven at 350 degrees F for 45 minutes.

Yield: 8 8-oz jars.

# Cream Cheese Cakes

*Cake:*

1 cup granulated sugar
1 1/2 cups all-purpose flour
1/3 cup cocoa
1 cup water
1 tablespoon vinegar
1/2 cup vegetable oil
1 teaspoon baking soda
1 teaspoon vanilla

*Filling:*
8 oz. cream cheese
1 egg
1/3 cup granulated sugar
8 oz. chocolate chips

In a large bowl, combine sugar, flour, cocoa, water, vinegar, oil, baking soda and vanilla to make the chocolate cake mixture. Beat until smooth.

In another bowl, combine cream cheese, egg and sugar and mix with electric mixer to make the cream cheese filling. Stir in chocolate chips.

Fill glass jars half full of the chocolate cake mixture. Top with the cream cheese filling. Place the filled jars on a baking sheet, not touching each other. Bake in a preheated oven at 350 degrees F for 16 to 17 minutes.

Yield: 12 8-oz. glass jars.

# Oreo Cheesecakes

This is my family's favorite recipe from the book. Makes up quickly and easily and disappears just as fast! I use a mallet to crush the cookies very small.

28 Oreo cookies, crushed
2 tablespoons butter or margarine, melted
2 pkg. (8 oz. each) cream cheese, softened
1/2 cup granulated sugar
1/2 teaspoon vanilla
1/2 cup sour cream
2 eggs

Spray jars with non-stick cooking spray, spraying well on the very bottom. Set aside 1/3 of the cookie crumbs. Mix remaining cookie crumbs and butter. Sprinkle onto bottom of glass jars.

In a large bowl, with an electric mixer, mix cream cheese, sugar and vanilla. Add sour cream; mix well. Add eggs and beat just until well blended. Add remaining cookies into batter. Pour batter evenly over crust in jars; top with additional chopped cookies, if desired.

Place the filled jars on a baking sheet, not touching each other. Bake in a preheated oven at 325 degrees F for 15 to 20 minutes. (watch closely) Cool completely. Refrigerate for 4 hours before serving.

Yield: 8 8-oz. jars

# Cherry Kuchen

1/2 cup butter
1/4 cup granulated sugar
1 egg yolk
1 1/4 cups all-purpose flour
1 teaspoon salt
1 tablespoon sugar

Cream butter, sugar and egg yolk together with a spoon. Add flour, salt and sugar; mix well. Spray glass jars with non-stick cooking spray. Divide the crust batter evenly into jars.

*Filling:*

1 can (14.5 oz.) sour cherries
3 tablespoons cornstarch

Drain the cherry juice into a small saucepan and set aside. Add the 3 tablespoons of cornstarch to a little water. Add 1/2 cup of sugar to the cherry juice, and add the cornstarch and water mixture. Cook the juice over medium heat until thick. Remove from heat and mix the can of cherries in with the juice. Divide the cherries with the thickened juice evenly into jars on top of crust batter.

*Topping:*

3/4 cup granulated sugar

2 tablespoons cream
2 eggs, beaten

Mix all the topping ingredients and pour over cherries. Place the filled jars on a baking sheet, not touching each other. Bake in a preheated oven at 350 degrees F for 20 minutes, then lower oven to 325 degrees F for 20 to 30 minutes longer. Serve with whipped cream, if desired.

Yield: 12 8-oz. glass jars.

# Chocolate Chip Pound Cakes

1 1/2 cups all-purpose flour
1/4 teaspoon salt
1/8 teaspoon baking soda
1 1/4 cups granulated sugar
1/2 cup butter, softened
3 eggs
2/3 cups sour cream
1/2 teaspoon vanilla extract
1 cup semi-sweet chocolate chips

In a medium bowl, combine flour, salt and baking soda; set aside. With an electric mixer, in a large bowl, cream together sugar and butter or margarine. Add eggs and mix well. Mix in sour cream and vanilla extract. Slowly add flour mixture and mix with whisk or spoon. Gently stir in chocolate chips.

Spray jars with non-stick cooking spray. Fill each jar 1/3 full of batter. Place the filled jars on a baking sheet, not touching each other and bake in a preheated oven at 350 degrees F for 45 to 50 minutes or until toothpick comes out clean.

Yield: 12 8-oz. glass jars.

# Key Lime Pie

*Graham Cracker Crust:*

3/4 cup graham cracker crumbs
2 tablespoons and 2 teaspoons packed brown sugar
3 tablespoons butter, melted

In a small bowl, stir together the graham cracker crumbs and sugar. Add butter and mix well. Spoon about 2 level tablespoons of mixture into the bottom of each jar. Refrigerate jars until ready for use.


3 eggs, separated
1/2 cup lime juice
1 (14-ounce) can sweetened condensed milk
6 drops green food coloring, optional
1/2 teaspoon cream of tartar
1/3 cup granulated sugar

In a medium bowl, beat egg yolks; mix in lime juice, sweetened condensed milk, and food coloring. Pour into glass jars. In small bowl, beat egg whites with cream of tartar until soft peaks are formed; slowly add sugar and beat until stiff. Spread on top of jars, sealing carefully to edge of jar. Place the filled jars on a baking sheet, not touching each other. Bake in a preheated oven at 350 degrees F for 12 to 15 minutes or until golden brown. Cool. Refrigerate for 3 hours or until set.

Yield: 4 8-oz. glass jars.

# Strawberry Shortcakes

1 1/4 cups all-purpose flour
3/4 cup granulated sugar
1/3 cup butter or margarine, softened
2/3 cup milk
2 eggs
2 1/2 teaspoons baking powder
1/2 teaspoon salt
Strawberries

In small bowl, with an electric mixer, combine flour, sugar, butter or margarine, milk, eggs, baking powder and salt. Beat at medium speed for 1 to 2 minutes or until well combined, scraping bowl often.

Spray jars with non-stick cooking spray. Divide the batter evenly into jars. Place the filled jars on a baking sheet, not touching each other. Bake in a preheated oven at 400 degrees F for 15 to 20 minutes or until lightly browned. Let cool. Serve with *Sweetened Whipped Cream* and strawberries.

Yield: 8 8-oz. glass jars.

*Sweetened Whipped Cream:*

1 cup heavy cream

3 tablespoons confectioners' sugar
1/2 teaspoon vanilla

In a large bowl, beat cream with an electric mixer until soft peaks are formed. Add confectioners' sugar and vanilla and beat until well mixed.

# Layered Pralines and Crème

*Crunch Mixture:*

1/2 cup bite-size crispy rice cereal squares
1/2 cup flaked coconut
1/2 cup slivered almonds
1/2 cup firmly packed brown sugar
1/2 cup chopped pecans
1/4 cup butter or margarine, melted

*Custard:*

1/2 cup granulated sugar
1 cup milk
1 egg, slightly beaten
1 tablespoon cornstarch
1 teaspoon vanilla
1 cup whipping cream, whipped

In a large bowl, mix together rice cereal squares, coconut, almonds, brown sugar and pecans. Pour melted butter or margarine on mixture; stir well to coat. Spread mixture out on a large cookie sheet. Bake in a preheated oven at 325 degrees F for 12 to 14 minutes, stirring occasionally, until golden brown. Cool completely; crumble cereal with fingers.

In a 2-quart saucepan, combine granulated sugar, milk, egg and cornstarch. Cook over medium heat, stirring often, until mixture comes to a full boil (7 to 9 minutes). Boil 1 minute. Remove from heat; stir in vanilla. Cover surface with plastic wrap; refrigerate 1 to 2 hours or until completely cooled. Fold whipped cream into custard mixture. Just before serving, alternate layers of custard and crunch mixture into glass jars.

Yield: 12 8-oz. glass jars.

# Red Velvet Cakes

2 cups all-purpose flour
1/3 cup unsweetened cocoa powder
1/2 teaspoon salt
3/4 teaspoon baking soda
3/4 cup and 2 teaspoons butter, softened
1 3/4 cups granulated sugar
3 eggs
1/3 cup and 1 tablespoon milk
3/4 cup and 2 teaspoons sour cream
3/4 (1 oz.) bottle red food coloring
1 1/2 teaspoons vanilla extract

In a bowl, combine flour, cocoa powder, salt and baking soda; set aside. With an electric mixer, beat butter and sugar in a large bowl for 5 minutes on medium speed. Add the eggs, one at a time, beating after each addition. Mix in milk, sour cream, food coloring and vanilla. Slowly add flour mixture, beating on low speed until just blended.

Spray jars with non-stick cooking spray. Fill each jar 1/4 to 1/3 full of batter. Place the filled jars on a baking sheet, not touching each other. Bake in a preheated oven at 350 degrees F for 20 minutes or until inserted toothpick comes out clean.

*Assembly:*

Remove jars from oven. Let cool for 10 minutes. After removing jars from oven, make Cream Cheese Frosting.

Using a large spoon, scoop out the top half of the cake in each jar (in one piece, if possible). Set aside.

Spoon a heaping tablespoon of Cream Cheese Frosting into each jar, covering the cake. Replace the top half of the cake into the jar. Top the jar off with the remaining frosting.

Yield: 12 8-oz. glass jars.

*Cream Cheese Frosting*

1/2 cup butter or margarine, softened
1 (8 oz.) package cream cheese, softened
1 (16 oz.) package confectioners' sugar
1 teaspoon vanilla extract

In a medium bowl, mix together butter or margarine and cream cheese; beat until smooth. Add sugar and vanilla; beat until fluffy and light.
Yield: 3 cups.

# Chocolate Cinnamon Cakes in a Jar

1 cup all-purpose flour
1 cup granulated sugar
1/4 cup butter or margarine
1/4 cup vegetable oil
3 tablespoons unsweetened cocoa powder
1/2 cup water
1/4 cup buttermilk
1 teaspoon cinnamon
1/2 teaspoon vanilla
1/2 teaspoon baking soda
1/2 teaspoon salt
2 eggs

In a large bowl, mix flour and sugar. In a saucepan, mix butter or margarine, oil, cocoa powder, and water; bring to a boil. Pour hot mixture over flour mixture; mix well. Add buttermilk, cinnamon and vanilla. Add baking soda, salt and eggs. Beat until well blended.

Spray jars with non-stick cooking spray. Fill each jar 1/3 full of batter. Place the filled jars on a baking sheet, not touching each other. Bake in preheated oven at 350 degrees F for 15 to 20 minutes or until inserted toothpick comes out clean.

*Assembly:*

Remove jars from oven. Let cool for 10 minutes. After removing jars from oven, make frosting.

Using a large spoon, scoop out the top half of the cake in each jar (in one piece, if possible). Set aside.

Spoon a heaping tablespoon of frosting into each jar, covering the cake. Replace the top half of the cake into the jar.

Top the jar off with the remaining frosting.

Yield: 10 to 12 8-oz. glass jars.


Frosting:

2 tablespoons butter or margarine, melted
2 tablespoons unsweetened cocoa powder
2 tablespoons buttermilk
1/4 teaspoon vanilla
1 1/2 cups confectioners' sugar

Mix butter or margarine, cocoa powder, buttermilk, vanilla and sugar. Add more milk if needed for thinning. Frost cakes in jars and garnish with cinnamon sugar or cocoa.

# Blueberry Pudding Cakes

1 cup fresh or frozen blueberries
2 eggs, separated
2/3 cup milk
1/4 cup lemon juice
1 teaspoon grated lemon peel
1 cup granulated sugar
1/4 cup all-purpose flour
1/4 teaspoon salt

Spray glass jars with non-stick cooking spray. Divide the blueberries evenly into the jars.

In a medium bowl, beat egg whites on high speed with electric mixer until stiff; set aside. In another bowl, whisk egg yolks slightly. Add milk, lemon juice and lemon peel. Mix in sugar, flour and salt; stir until smooth. Add to beaten egg whites. Pour over blueberries in jars.

Place jars without touching in an oblong pan, 9x13x2 inches, on a rack; pour very hot water into pan until 1 inch deep. Bake in a preheated oven at 350 degrees F 30 to 35 minutes or until golden brown (watch carefully). Remove jars from water. Serve cake warm or cool with *Lemon Whipped Cream*.

Yield: 8 8-oz. glass jars.

*Lemon Whipped Cream:*

1 cup whipping cream
1/4 cup granulated sugar
3 teaspoons lemon juice
1/2 tablespoon lemon zest

Beat whipping cream on high speed to soft peaks. Add sugar, lemon juice and zest and continue beating until smooth. Refrigerate until ready to use.

# Cranberry Cake with Hot Butter Sauce

3 teaspoons butter, melted
1 cup granulated sugar
1/2 cup water
1/2 cup evaporated milk
2 cups all-purpose flour
1 teaspoon salt
1 teaspoon baking soda
2 cups raw cranberries

Mix butter, sugar, water and milk together. Add the flour, salt, baking soda and cranberries. Pour evenly into glass jars.

Place the filled jars on a baking sheet, not touching each other. Bake in a preheated oven at 325 degrees F for 20 to 30 minutes or until passes the toothpick test. Poke holes in cake with toothpick, fork or chopstick. Pour *Hot Butter Sauce* over cake in jars.

*Hot Butter Sauce:*
1/2 cup butter
1 cup sugar
1 teaspoon vanilla
1/2 cup evaporated milk

Mix all ingredients together in a saucepan and bring to boil. Pour evenly over cranberry cake in jars.

Yield: 8 8-oz. jars

# Tres Leches Cakes

This is a very moist cake that will need to be refrigerated. This recipe will fill a lot of jars, about 16, depending on the size and how full they are filled. I actually scooped cake out of the jars and added some of the whipped cream topping to the center, then replaced the cake on top and added more whipped topping. But since the cake is so moist, it was kind of messy. Next time I will just add the whipped topping to the top of the cake.

*Cake:*

2 teaspoons baking powder
2 cups all-purpose flour
1 teaspoon salt
6 large eggs, room temperature
1 1/3 cups granulated sugar
1/2 cup whole milk
1 tablespoon vanilla extract

*Tres Leches:*

1 14-oz. can sweetened condensed milk
1 cup heavy cream
2/3 cup evaporated milk

*Topping:*

1/2 teaspoon vanilla extract

1 cup heavy whipping cream
Toasted coconut

*Cake:*

In a medium bowl, mix together baking powder, flour and salt. Separate eggs, placing egg whites in another large mixing bowl. Beat egg whites until soft and fluffy peaks form. Using an electric mixer, gradually beat in sugar. Beat in all 6 egg yolks one at a time; beat well after each yolk is added. Alternate beating in the flour mixture and whole milk, being sure to start and end with flour mixture. Beat in the vanilla extract.

Spray jars with non-stick cooking spray. Fill each jar 1/4 to 1/3 full of batter. Place the filled jars on a baking sheet, not touching each other. Bake in preheated oven at 350 degrees F for 15 to 20 minutes or until inserted toothpick comes out clean. Let cool for at least ten minutes.

*Tres Leches:*

Set aside 2 tablespoons of sweetened condensed milk for topping. In a large mixing bowl, whisk together the remainder of sweetened condensed milk, heavy cream and evaporated milk. Pour mixture into large measuring cup. Using a fork, wooden toothpick or wooden skewer, poke several holes into each cake in a jar, be sure the holes go all the way to the bottom of the jar.

Place 1 tablespoon of tres leches mixture on top of each cake in a jar. Each little cake should hold approximately 3 tablespoons of tres leches mixture. Be sure to let 1 tablespoon of mixture soak into the cake completely before adding another. Cover jars with plastic wrap or jar lid and place in refrigerator for four hours or overnight.

*Topping:*

In a small mixing bowl, beat heavy cream until stiff peaks start to form. Gently fold in the remaining two tablespoons of sweetened condensed milk and 1/2 teaspoon vanilla. When ready to serve, place a dollop of topping on top of the cake in each jar and sprinkle with toasted coconut.

Yield: 16 8-oz. jars

# White Chocolate Bread Pudding

8 cups day old French bread, torn into small pieces
1/2 cup dried cherries, raisins or dried cranberries
4 oz. white chocolate baking chips
1 (14-ounce) can sweetened condensed milk
2 1/2 cups water
3 eggs, beaten
2 tablespoons lemon juice
2 tablespoons margarine or butter, melted
1 tablespoon brown sugar
1/8 teaspoon ground nutmeg

Spray glass jars with non-stick cooking spray. Melt chocolate in microwave for 30 seconds. If not completely melted, continue melting, stirring every 15 seconds until melted.

In another large bowl, combine melted white chocolate, condensed milk, water, eggs, lemon juice and margarine or butter; add bread cubes and dried fruit and mix until bread is completely moistened. (Press bread down with spoon, if necessary, to moisten completely.) Divide the mixture into 8 glass jars. Combine brown sugar and nutmeg and sprinkle on top.

Place jars without touching in oblong pan, 9x13x2 inches, on a rack; pour very hot water into pan until 1 inch deep or at least an inch up the sides of the glass jars. Bake in a preheated oven at 350 degrees F for 30 to 40 minutes or until a knife inserted in the center comes out clean. (watch carefully) Remove jars from water. Serve warm or let cool. Refrigerate.

Yield: 8 8-oz. glass jars.

# Peanut Butter Cakes

1 3/4 cups all-purpose flour
1 1/4 cups brown sugar, firmly packed
1 cup milk
1/3 cup margarine
1/3 cup peanut butter
3 teaspoons baking powder
1 teaspoon salt
1 teaspoon vanilla
2 eggs
12 miniature milk chocolate-covered peanut butter cups

In a large bowl, combine flour, brown sugar, milk, margarine, peanut butter, baking powder, salt, vanilla and eggs. With an electric mixer at low speed, beat until moistened; then beat 2 minutes at medium speed.

Spray jars with non-stick cooking spray. Fill each jar 1/3 full of batter. Insert a peanut butter cup into cake batter in each jar. Place the filled jars on a baking sheet, not touching each other. Bake in a preheated oven at 350 degrees F for 15 to 25 minutes or until cakes spring back when lightly touched.

Yield: 12 8-oz. glass jars.

# Molten Delight Cakes

2 tablespoons plus 3/4 cup butter, divided
8 oz. 62% cacao bittersweet chocolate baking bar, broken into pieces
3 large egg yolks
3 large eggs
1/4 cup plus 1 tablespoon granulated sugar
1 teaspoon vanilla extract
1 tablespoon all-purpose flour
Confectioners' sugar

Generously spray jars with non-stick cooking spray. In a medium pan, combine chocolate and 3/4 cup butter; stir over low heat until chocolate is melted and mixture is smooth. Remove from heat.

In a large bowl, with an electric mixer, mix eggs yolks, eggs, sugar and vanilla about 7 minutes or until thick. Fold in flour and mix until blended well. Spoon batter evenly into glass jars. Place the filled jars on a baking sheet, not touching each other. Bake in a preheated oven at 425 degrees F for 12 to 13 minutes or until sides are set and 1-inch centers move slightly when shaken. Sprinkle with confectioners' sugar.

Yield: 6 8-oz. glass jars.

# Carrot Cakes with Creamy Frosting

2 1/2 cups all-purpose flour
2 teaspoons baking soda
1 teaspoon salt
2 cups granulated sugar
2 eggs
1 cup vegetable oil
2 teaspoons vanilla
1 8 oz. can crushed pineapple, well drained
2 cups shredded carrots
1/2 cup chopped nuts
1/2 cup raisins

Spray jars with non-stick cooking spray. In medium bowl, combine flour, baking soda and salt; set aside. In another bowl, combine sugar, eggs, oil, and vanilla; beat well. Stir in flour mixture; mix well.

Stir in pineapple, carrots, nuts and raisins. Pour evenly into jars. Place the filled jars on a baking sheet, not touching each other. Bake in a preheated oven at 350 degrees F for 35 to 50 minutes or until cake springs back when touched lightly in center.

Assembly:

Remove jars from oven. Let cool for 10 minutes. After removing jars from oven, make Creamy Frosting.

Using a large spoon, scoop out the top half of the cake in each jar (in one piece, if possible). Set aside.

Spoon a heaping tablespoon of *Creamy Frosting* into each jar, covering the cake. Replace the top half of the cake into the jar.

Top the jar off with the remaining frosting.

Yield: 12 8-oz. glass jars.

*Creamy Frosting:*

2 1/2 cups confectioners' sugar
1 8 oz. pkg. cream cheese, softened
6 tablespoons margarine or butter, softened
2 teaspoons vanilla
1 cup coconut
1/2 cup chopped nuts

In a large bowl, combine confectioners' sugar, cream cheese, margarine or butter and vanilla; beat until smooth. Stir in coconut and nuts. Spread over cake in jars.

# Apple Pecan Layer Cakes

2 1/2 cups all-purpose flour
2 cups granulated sugar
1 teaspoon salt
1 teaspoon cinnamon
1 teaspoon baking powder
1 teaspoon baking soda
1 1/2 cups applesauce
3/4 cup vegetable oil
2 eggs
1/2 cup chopped pecans

Spray jars with non-stick cooking spray. In large bowl, mix flour, sugar, salt, cinnamon, baking powder and baking soda. Add applesauce, oil and eggs; beat at low speed just until well mixed. Beat for 2 minutes at high speed. Stir in pecans.

Pour batter into jars. Place the filled jars on a baking sheet, not touching each other. Bake in a preheated oven at 350 degrees F for 20 to 30 minutes or until toothpick inserted in center comes out clean.

*Assembly:*

Remove jars from oven. Let cool for 10 minutes. After removing jars from oven, make *Browned Butter Frosting*.

Using a large spoon, scoop out the top half of the cake in each jar (in one piece, if possible). Set aside.

Spoon a heaping tablespoon of Browned Butter Frosting into each jar, covering the cake. Replace the top half of the cake into the jar.

Top the jar off with the remaining frosting.

Yield: 12 8-oz. glass jars.

*Browned Butter Frosting:*

4 1/2 cups confectioners' sugar
1/2 cup butter (not margarine)
4 tablespoons apple juice

In a small heavy saucepan over medium heat, brown butter until light golden brown, stirring constantly. Remove from heat and let cool. In large bowl, mix confectioners' sugar, browned butter and apple juice; beat at low speed until well mixed and smooth.

# Chocolate Iced Shortbreads

1 cup margarine or butter, softened
1/2 cup granulated sugar
1 teaspoon vanilla extract
2 cups all-purpose flour
1 3/4 cups mini semi-sweet chocolate morsels, divided
Chocolate frosting (below)

Spray jars well with non-stick cooking spray. In a bowl, cream butter or margarine, sugar and vanilla until light and fluffy. Add flour; mix to form stiff dough. Stir in 1 cup mini chocolate morsels. Press dough into prepared jars. Place the filled jars on a baking sheet, not touching each other. Bake in a preheated oven at 350 degrees F for 13 to 15 minutes or until firm. Cool. Spread with *Chocolate Frosting*; sprinkle with remaining 3/4 cup mini chocolate morsels.

Yield: 12 8-oz. glass jars.


*Chocolate Frosting:*

1 cup semi-sweet chocolate chips
1 (14 oz.) can sweetened condensed milk
1/8 teaspoon salt
2 cups confectioners' sugar
1 teaspoon vanilla extract

In a medium saucepan, mix together chocolate chips, condensed milk and salt. Cook and stir on medium heat until chocolate chips melt; cook and stir 3 minutes more. Remove from heat; let cool for 15 minutes. With electric mixer on medium, beat in confectioners' sugar and vanilla extract until smooth and creamy.

# Orange Zucchini Cakes

3/4 cup vegetable oil
3/4 cup granulated sugar
2 eggs
2 tablespoons orange liqueur
1/2 teaspoon vanilla
3/4 teaspoon grated orange rind
1 1/2 cups all-purpose flour
1 teaspoon baking soda
1 teaspoon cinnamon
1/2 teaspoon baking powder
1/4 + 1/8 teaspoon salt
1 cup zucchini, grated
1/2 cup walnuts, chopped
1/2 cup dates, finely chopped

In a large bowl, beat together oil and sugar with an electric mixer. Add eggs, beating after each egg addition. Add liqueur, vanilla and orange rind. Mix flour, baking soda, cinnamon, baking powder and salt and add to batter. Stir in zucchini, walnuts and dates.

Spray jars with non-stick cooking spray. Fill each jar 1/3 full of batter. Place the filled jars on a baking sheet, not touching each other. Bake in preheated oven at 375 degrees F for 20 to 25 minutes. Frost with *Orange Frosting*.

Yield: 10 to 12 8-oz. glass jars.

*Orange Frosting:*

1/2 cup butter, softened
1 (8 oz.) package cream cheese, softened
2 cups confectioners' sugar
2 tablespoons orange liqueur
1 tablespoon grated orange rind
1 teaspoon vanilla

Beat all ingredients together until smooth with electric mixer. Spread on cakes in jars.

# Applesauce Cupcakes in a Jar

1 cup granulated sugar
1/2 cup vegetable oil
1 egg
1 cup applesauce
1 1/2 cups all-purpose flour
1/2 teaspoon cinnamon
1/2 teaspoon nutmeg
1/4 teaspoon salt
1 teaspoon baking soda dissolved in 1 tablespoon hot water
1/2 cup chopped raisins and nuts

Mix ingredients together in order given.

Spray jars with non-stick cooking spray. Fill each jar 1/3 full of batter. Place the filled jars on a baking sheet, not touching each other. Bake in preheated oven at 350 degrees F for 17 to 20 minutes or until a toothpick inserted in the center comes out clean. Keep refrigerated.

*Assembly:*

Remove jars from oven. Let cool for 10 minutes. After removing jars from oven, make *Pineapple-Cream Cheese Frosting*.

Using a large spoon, scoop out the top half of the cake in each jar (in one piece, if possible). Set aside.

Spoon a heaping tablespoon of Pineapple-Cream Cheese Frosting into each jar, covering the cake. Replace the top half of the cake into the jar.

Top the jar off with the remaining frosting.

Yield: 12 8-oz. glass jars.

*Pineapple-Cream Cheese Frosting:*

1 (8 oz.) can crushed pineapple
1 (8 oz.) package cream cheese, softened
1/4 cup butter or margarine, softened
1 (16 oz.) package confectioners' sugar

Drain pineapple and put into a sieve or strainer. Push pineapple against the sieve to force out additional juice; set aside. With an electric mixer at medium speed, beat cream cheese and butter until fluffy; gradually stir in confectioners' sugar and pineapple.

Yield: 3 cups.

# Spice Crumb Cakes

2 cups all-purpose flour
1 cup brown sugar, firmly packed
1/2 cup margarine or butter, melted
1 teaspoon baking powder
1/2 teaspoon baking soda
1/4 teaspoon salt
1 teaspoon cinnamon
1/4 teaspoon cloves
1 cup buttermilk
1 egg
1 teaspoon vanilla

Spray jars with non-stick cooking spray. In a bowl, combine flour, brown sugar and butter or margarine; mix with fork until mixture resembles coarse crumbs. Remove 1 cup crumbs; set aside. Add baking powder, baking soda, salt, cinnamon and cloves to mixture in bowl; stir with fork to blend well.

In a small bowl, combine buttermilk, egg and vanilla; mix well. Add to flour mixture and stir until well mixed. Divide mixture evenly among jars. Sprinkle reserved crumb mixture over top of batter in each jar. Place the filled jars on a baking sheet, not touching each other. Bake in a preheated oven at 350 degrees F for 25 to 40 minutes or until toothpick inserted in center comes out clean. Serve warm or cool.

Yield: 12 8-oz. glass jars.

# Cranberry Cobbler

2 1/4 cups fresh cranberries
1/4 cup granulated sugar
1/3 cup coarsely chopped pecans
6 tablespoons melted butter, divided
1 egg, beaten
1/2 teaspoon vanilla
1/2 cup sugar
1/2 cup all-purpose flour
Ice cream or whipped cream

Spray jars with non-stick cooking spray. Spread cranberries evenly over bottom of jars. Combine 1/4 cup sugar, pecans, and 4 tablespoons butter. Pour over cranberries. Combine egg, vanilla, sugar, flour, and 2 tablespoons butter until flour is moistened. Spread evenly over cranberries.

Place filled jars on a baking sheet, not touching each other. Bake in preheated 350 degrees F oven for 30 to 40 minutes. Serve, topped with ice cream or whipped cream.

Yield: 8 8-oz. glass jars.

# Chocolate Cupcakes in a Jar

3/4 cup vegetable oil
1 1/4 cups granulated sugar
2 eggs
1 teaspoon vanilla extract
1 cup milk
1 3/4 cups all-purpose flour
1/2 cup unsweetened cocoa powder
1 teaspoon baking soda
1/2 teaspoon salt
1 3/4 cups mini semi-sweet chocolate chips
Confectioners' sugar - optional

In a large bowl, beat vegetable oil and granulated sugar until light and fluffy. Add eggs and vanilla; beat well. Add milk. Mix together flour, cocoa powder, baking soda and salt. Add flour mixture to sugar mixture; beat well. Add the chocolate chips and mix well.

Spray jars with non-stick cooking spray. Fill each jar 1/4 to 1/3 full of batter. Place the filled jars on a baking sheet, not touching each other. Bake in preheated oven at 375 degrees F for 20 to 25 minutes or until inserted toothpick comes out clean. Frost with *Chocolate Frosting* or sprinkle confectioners' sugar over top of cakes.

Yield: 12 8-oz. glass jars.

*Chocolate Frosting:*

1 cup semi-sweet chocolate chips
1 (14 oz.) can sweetened condensed milk
1/8 teaspoon salt
2 cups confectioners' sugar
1 teaspoon vanilla extract

In a medium saucepan, mix together chocolate chips, condensed milk and salt. Cook and stir on medium heat until chocolate chips melt; cook and stir 3 minutes more. Remove from heat; let cool for 15 minutes. With electric mixer on medium, beat in confectioners' sugar and vanilla extract until smooth and creamy. Yield: 1 1/2 cups.

# Apple Crisp

*Also make Peach Crisp with this recipe by using peaches instead of apples.*

4 cups peeled, cored, apples, sliced into small pieces
1 teaspoon cinnamon
1/2 teaspoon salt
1/4 cup water
3/4 cup all-purpose flour
1 cup granulated sugar
6 tablespoons butter
Whipping cream, whipped, or vanilla ice cream, optional

Spray jars with non-stick cooking spray. Arrange apples in bottom of jars. Sprinkle with cinnamon, salt, and water. Combine flour, sugar, and butter with pastry cutter. Mix until consistency of coarse meal. Sprinkle mixture over apples.

Place the filled jars on a baking sheet, not touching each other. Bake in preheated 350 degrees F oven for 25 to 35 minutes. Serve warm with whipped cream or ice cream if desired.

Yield: 6 to 8 8-oz. glass jars.

# Chocolate Pumpkin Muffins

1 1/2 cups all-purpose flour
1/2 cup granulated sugar
2 teaspoons baking powder
1/2 teaspoon salt
1/2 teaspoon cinnamon
1/2 cup solid pack canned pumpkin
1 cup milk
1 egg
1/4 cup butter or margarine, melted
1 cup semi-sweet chocolate chips
1/4 cup finely chopped nuts

In a large bowl, mix together flour, sugar, baking powder, salt and cinnamon. In another bowl, combine pumpkin, milk, egg and butter or margarine; add to flour mixture. Add chocolate chips; stir until dry ingredients are just moistened. Spoon into jars, filling each 1/2 full. Sprinkle 1 teaspoon nuts over each jar.

Place the filled jars on a baking sheet, not touching each other. Bake in a preheated oven at 400 degrees F for 13 to 15 minutes.

Yield: 4 8-oz. glass jars.

# Lemon Pudding Cakes

3 tablespoons unsalted butter or margarine, at room temperature
1/2 cup granulated sugar
2 large eggs, separated
1/4 cup lemon juice
1/3 cup all-purpose flour
1 cup milk
1 teaspoon vanilla extract
2 teaspoons finely grated lemon rind
2 tablespoons confectioners' sugar

Spray jars with non-stick cooking spray. In a large bowl, beat the butter or margarine with an electric mixer at high speed until creamy, about 2 minutes. Add 1/3 cup of granulated sugar, a little at a time, beating after each addition. Continue beating at high speed until fluffy - about 2 minutes.

One at a time, add egg yolks and beat at medium speed after each addition only until just mixed. Beat in the lemon juice, then the flour, and continue beating at medium speed for 2 minutes. Add the milk, vanilla and lemon rind; beat only until just mixed.

Clean the beaters. In a medium bowl, beat the egg whites at high speed until frothy. Add the remaining granulated sugar slowly while beating; continue beating until stiff peaks form. Fold the egg whites into the batter.

Spoon the mixture into glass jars. Place jars without touching in a baking dish with 2" sides. Pour enough hot water into the baking dish to come 1/3 to 1/2 of the way up the sides of the jars. Bake in a preheated oven at 350 degrees F, in the hot water bath for 30 to 35 minutes or until puffed and golden. Sprinkle confectioners' sugar on the tops of cakes and serve warm or chilled.

Yield: 4 8-oz. glass jars.

# Coconut Pecan Cakes

2 cups granulated sugar
2 cups all-purpose flour
1 1/2 cups butter or margarine, softened
1 cup buttermilk
4 eggs
1 teaspoon baking soda
1/2 teaspoon salt
1 tablespoon vanilla
2 cups flaked coconut
1 cup chopped pecans

In a large bowl, combine sugar, flour, butter or margarine, buttermilk, eggs, baking soda, salt and vanilla. Beat at low speed, scraping bowl often, until all ingredients are moistened. Beat at high speed for 3 to 4 minutes or until smooth. By hand, stir in coconut and pecans.

Spray jars with non-stick cooking spray. Divide the batter evenly into jars. Place the filled jars on a baking sheet, not touching each other. Bake in a preheated oven at 350 degrees F for 35 to 40 minutes or until center of cake is firm to the touch and edges begin to pull away from sides of jars.

*Assembly:*

Remove jars from oven. Let cool for 10 minutes. After removing jars from oven, make frosting.

Using a large spoon, scoop out the top half of the cake in each jar (in one piece, if possible). Set aside.

Spoon a heaping tablespoon of frosting into each jar, covering the cake. Replace the top half of the cake into the jar.

Top the jar off with the remaining frosting.

Yield: 20 8-oz. glass jars.

*Frosting:*

1/3 cup butter or margarine
3 cups confectioners' sugar
1 1/2 teaspoons vanilla
1 to 3 tablespoons milk

In a saucepan, heat 1/3 cup butter over medium heat, stirring constantly, until delicate brown, 5 to 6 minutes. In a small bowl, combine melted butter, confectioners' sugar, vanilla and 1 tablespoon milk. Beat at medium speed, adding more milk if necessary, scraping bowl often, until frosting is spreadable and smooth.

# NO-BAKE DESSERTS

## Whipped Cream Concoctions

Moms and Grandmas have been making whipped cream topping forever. There's certainly nothing wrong with a swirl of plain whipped cream to garnish your dessert, but today's taste buds are a little more sophisticated than ho-hum whipped cream with a dash of vanilla.

With so many extracts and flavorings available at markets and specialty shops, there are almost unlimited variations that can take your whipped cream to a new gastronomic level. You can match your whipped cream to your dessert's main flavoring, or add a complementary taste to add to the complexity of the recipe's flavors.

Tips and Recipes

Don't leave whipped cream sitting out at room temperature. If it does become warm and greasy, it can be re-whipped several times to reinflate it.

Add approximately four ounces of cream cheese to two cups heavy cream. Not only does it add flavor, but it also helps the whipped cream remain firm. Don't care to add cream cheese flavor? Add only one ounce of cream cheese per cup of cream to maintain the whipped firmness without the cheesy taste. Cream the sugar and cream cheese together first to eliminate lumps. If you use a higher ratio of cream cheese to cream, you can use the spread as a pastry filling.

For a change of pace, use brown sugar instead of white sugar when making whipped cream. The tiny brown flecks add a little bit of texture and are every bit as sweet as standard white sugar.

Berry Whipped Cream

Beat 1/3 cup sugar with four ounces of cream cheese. Add two cups whipping cream and beat until it forms soft peaks. Add one drop of red food coloring and one teaspoon of strawberry or raspberry flavoring. This is great as a topping, and it's good in fruit desserts that call for whipped cream.

Caramel Whipped Cream

Use brown sugar and add two teaspoons of caramel flavoring to your whipped cream. This is great on any chocolate dessert recipe.

Brown Sugar Cinnamon Whipped Cream

Use brown sugar instead of white sugar, and add a teaspoon of cinnamon while whipping your cream. You can also use brown sugar flavoring to intensify the flavor.

Nutty Caramel Whipped Cream

Add approximately one cup coarsely chopped nuts to your caramel whipped cream recipe for a nutty-caramel treat.

The nuts will become soft after a few hours, so plan on using it soon after preparing it.

## Butterscotch Whipped Cream

Use brown sugar in place of white sugar and add two teaspoons butterscotch flavoring to your whipped cream. A sprinkling of ground pecans on your dessert topping looks great and adds a bit of crunch.

## Citrus Whipped Cream

Lemon, lime or orange zest adds flecks of color, as well as a hint of citrus flavor. Top a lemon cake or a key lime pie with one of these colorful whipped cream toppings. For even more citrus flavor, add lemon, lime or orange flavoring along with the zest. Generally, two teaspoons is enough to add a tangy snap of citrus to your topping.

## Chocolate Whipped Cream

Whip cream until you create soft peaks. Melt 1/2 cup chocolate or semi-sweet chocolate chips. Allow the liquid to cool, but not harden. Stir 1/3rd of the whipped cream into the chocolate, add 1/2 teaspoon vanilla and sugar into the mixture. Stir the resulting mixture into the whipped cream and continue beating until it reaches the desired consistency.

## Chocolate Whipped Cream II

Use three tablespoons of dark cocoa powder and two ounces cream cheese to create a smooth and silky milk chocolate topping. Use approximately two cups of heavy cream and 1/2 teaspoon vanilla extract, along with 1/2 cup sugar.

## Peanut Butter Whipped Cream

Whip two cups whipping cream, along with brown sugar and 1/3 cup peanut butter. This works best with a stand mixer and a whisk attachment. When your topping has stiff peaks, fold in 1/3 cup coarsely chopped salted nuts. The nuts will grow soggy after a few hours, so add the nuts just before you're ready to serve your dessert.

# Pumpkin Mousse

1 envelope unflavored gelatin
1/2 cup granulated sugar
2 large eggs
1/8 teaspoon salt
1/4 cup cold water
1 cup fresh or canned pumpkin puree
3/4 teaspoon ground cinnamon
1/2 teaspoon ground ginger
1/4 teaspoon allspice
1/4 teaspoon ground nutmeg
3 cups frozen whipped dessert topping, thawed, or 1 1/2 cups heavy cream, whipped

*Optional garnishes:*
1 cup frozen whipped dessert topping, thawed or 1/2 cup heavy cream, whipped

Place the gelatin, sugar, eggs, salt, and water in a small saucepan, and beat until smooth. Cook, stirring constantly, over moderately low heat until the sugar and gelatin dissolve and the mixture thickens slightly - about 5 minutes. (Do not boil.) Remove from heat; set in a large container of cold water. Stir occasionally and leave the mixture in cold water until it cools to lukewarm.

Mix in pumpkin, cinnamon, ginger, allspice and nutmeg. Refrigerate for 15 minutes; fold in whipped topping. Pour into glass jars. Refrigerate for 4 hours or overnight. Just before serving, add whipped topping.

Yield: 6 or 8 8-oz. glass jars.

# Whipped Chocolate Delight

*Graham Cracker Crust:*

3/4 cup graham cracker crumbs
2 tablespoons and 2 teaspoons packed brown sugar
2 tablespoons and 2 teaspoons unsweetened cocoa powder
3 tablespoons butter, melted

In a small bowl, stir together the graham cracker crumbs and sugar. Add butter and mix well. Add cocoa powder. Press about 2 level tablespoons of mixture into the bottom of each jar. Refrigerate jars until ready for use.

1 1/2 packages (8 oz. each) cream cheese, room temperature
3 tablespoons granulated sugar
1 cup heavy cream
1/2 cup Hershey's Spreads - Chocolate
1/3 cup chocolate chips

Using an electric mixer, beat cream cheese and sugar until smooth. Reduce the mixer speed to low and gradually add one cup of heavy cream. Increase the speed to high and beat until thick and stiff, about 2 minutes. Fold in Hershey's chocolate spreads and stir until well mixed.

Remove jars from refrigerator. Layer jars with cream cheese batter, chocolate chips and more cream cheese batter. Top with *Chocolate Whipped Cream*. Refrigerate for at least 1 hour before serving.

*Chocolate Whipped Cream*:

1 cup whipping cream
1/4 teaspoon vanilla extract
1/4 cup granulated sugar
1/4 cup semi-sweet chocolate chips

Whip the cream with electric mixer until soft peaks form. Stir vanilla extract and sugar into the whipped cream.

Melt chocolate in microwave for one minute at high heat, remove and stir until completely melted. Let the chocolate cool for 3 minutes. The chocolate should be warm but not hot. Stir 1/4 of the whipped cream into the chocolate. Stir the chocolate mixture into the remaining whipped cream.

Yield: 8 8-oz. jars

# Peach-Raspberry Mousse

1 (3 oz.) package peach-flavored gelatin
1 cup water
1/2 cup sour cream
1 teaspoon lemon juice
1/2 pint frozen peach sorbet
1 8 oz. pkg. frozen sliced peaches
1 10-oz. pkg. frozen whole raspberries

Cut each slice of frozen peaches into 3 or 4 pieces. Microwave at 50% power for 15 seconds or until they are still cold but no longer frozen.

Pour the gelatin into a large bowl. Heat the water in microwave until boiling and add to bowl. Stir until gelatin is dissolved. Add lemon juice and sour cream; whisk until smooth.

Using a tablespoon, spoon out the frozen sorbet and add in spoonfuls to the gelatin mixture. Stir until sorbet is melted. Add the peaches and frozen raspberries and stir until well mixed. Pour into 6 jars and refrigerate for at least 2 hours before serving. Add *Whipped Topping* before serving.

Yield: 6 8-oz. glass jars.

*Whipped Topping:*

1 cup heavy cream

1/4 cup granulated sugar
1 teaspoon vanilla extract

Chill the beaters and a mixing bowl in freezer for about 10 minutes. Beat whipping cream until thickened; beat in sugar and vanilla. Beat until soft peaks form; then beat about 2 minutes longer until stiff peaks form.

Yield: 2 cups.

# Frozen Mocha Dessert

1 1/2 cups chocolate wafer cookies, crushed (about 26 wafers)
1/4 cup margarine or butter, melted
1/4 cup granulated sugar
1 8 oz. pkg. cream cheese, softened
1 cup chocolate flavored syrup
1 14 oz. can sweetened condensed milk
1 to 2 tablespoons instant coffee
1 teaspoon hot water
1 cup (1/2 pint) whipping cream, whipped

Mix together crushed cookies, margarine or butter and sugar; divide evenly into jars. Shake jars a little to even out the crumbs.

In a bowl, beat cream cheese until light and fluffy. Slowly beat in chocolate syrup and condensed milk; beat until smooth. Mix coffee and water together; stir until coffee is dissolved and add to cream cheese mixture, mixing well. Stir in whipped cream. Divide mixture evenly among jars; cover. Freeze 6 hours or until firm. Store any leftovers in freezer.

Yield: 8 8-oz. glass jars.

# Chocolate Maple Nut Pudding

1 cup evaporated skim milk
1 package (6 ounces) chocolate chips
4 teaspoons maple extract or 1 teaspoon other extract
1/4 cup walnuts or pecans, coarsely chopped

Heat the milk in a small saucepan over low heat for about 5 minutes or until little bubbles appear near the sides of the saucepan. Place the chocolate chips and maple extract in an electric blender, pour in the hot milk, and whirl at high speed for about 3 minutes or until the chocolate chips melt and the mixture is smooth.

Pour into glass jars, and refrigerate for several hours or until slightly thickened. Stir in walnuts before serving.

Yield: 4 8-oz. glass jars.

# No-Bake Strawberry Cheesecakes

*Graham Cracker Crust:*

3/4 cup graham cracker crumbs
2 tablespoons and 2 teaspoons packed brown sugar
3 tablespoons butter, melted

In a small bowl, stir together the graham cracker crumbs and sugar. Add butter and mix well. Put about 2 level tablespoons of mixture into the bottom of each jar. Refrigerate jars until ready for use.

*Cheesecake Batter:*

1 1/2 packages (8 oz. each) cream cheese, room temperature
3 tablespoons granulated sugar
1 cup heavy cream

*Whipped Cream:*

1 cup heavy cream
1/4 cup granulated sugar
1/4 teaspoon vanilla extract

*Other Ingredients:*

6 medium fresh strawberries, sliced into thin slices
3/4 cup strawberry jam

*Cheesecake Batter:* Put the cream cheese and sugar in a large bowl. Using an electric mixer, beat on medium high until smooth. Reduce mixer speed to low and gradually add one cup of heavy cream. Increase speed to high and beat until thick and stiff, about 2 minutes.

Remove jars from refrigerator. Top graham cracker crust with cheesecake batter, strawberries and jam, alternating red layers with cheesecake batter.

Whip the remaining cream with electric mixer until soft peaks form. Stir vanilla extract and sugar into the whipped cream. Add to the top of each jar. Refrigerate for at least 1 hour before serving.

Yield: 8 8-oz. jars.

# Frozen Pistachio Dessert

*Crust:*

1 cup (about 27) crushed vanilla wafers
1/2 cup finely chopped red pistachios
1/4 cup margarine or butter, melted

*Filling:*

2 3-oz. pkg. cream cheese, softened
3 1/2-oz. pkg. instant pistachio pudding mix
1 1/4 cups milk
2 cups frozen whipped topping, thawed
2 tablespoons chopped red pistachios

In a bowl, combine all crust ingredients; mix well. Add to the bottom of the glass jars. In a small bowl, beat cream cheese until light and fluffy. Add pudding mix and milk; beat until smooth. Fold whipped topping into cream cheese mixture; spoon into jars. Freeze 5 hours until firm or overnight. Add *Raspberry Whipped Topping* or *Pistachio Whipped Topping* to jars before serving. (recipes below) Sprinkle pistachios on top.

Yield: 8 8-oz. glass jars.

*Raspberry Whipped Cream:*

2 ounces cream cheese
3 tablespoons granulated sugar
1 cup whipping cream
1/2 teaspoon raspberry flavoring or extract
1 drop red food color

Beat cream cheese and sugar with electric mixer until blended well and the mixture is soft and consistent. Add whipping cream, flavoring or extract and food color. Beat until soft peaks form. Refrigerate until ready to use.


*Pistachio Whipped Cream:*
1 cup whipping cream
3/4 cup confectioners' sugar
1/2 pkg. instant pistachio pudding mix
1/2 teaspoon vanilla

Beat whipping cream until soft peaks form. Add pudding mix, confectioners' sugar and vanilla; beat until smooth. Refrigerate until ready to use.

# Cranberry Crunch Parfaits

2 tablespoons butter or margarine
1/4 cup quick-cooking oats
2 tablespoons pecans, chopped
2 tablespoons brown sugar
1/4 teaspoon ground cinnamon
1/2 cup granulated sugar
1/2 cup water
1 cup fresh cranberries
Vanilla ice cream

Melt butter or margarine in a small skillet. Add oats, pecans, brown sugar and cinnamon. Cook and stir over medium-high heat until mixture is brown and crumbly. Remove from heat; set aside.

In a medium saucepan, combine granulated sugar and water; stir until dissolved. Add cranberries. Boil until most of the skins have popped, about 5 to 10 minutes; cool.

In 3 glass jars, layer cooked cranberries and oat mixture. Add vanilla ice cream on top just before serving.

Yield: 3 8-oz. glass jars.

# Fresh Strawberry Trifle

12 ladyfingers, cut into pieces
1 quart fresh strawberries, cleaned, hulled and sliced
4 tablespoons dry sherry, divided
1/3 cup lemon juice
1 14-ounce can sweetened condensed milk
3 egg whites, stiffly beaten
1 cup (1/2 pint) whipping cream, whipped
Additional whipped cream, optional

Line bottom of glass jars with ladyfinger pieces. Divide 1 1/2 cups of sliced strawberries over ladyfingers in jars; sprinkle with 2 tablespoons sherry divided among jars. Set aside.

In a large bowl, mix lemon juice, sweetened condensed milk and 1 1/2 cups strawberries. Fold in egg whites, whipped cream and remaining 2 tablespoons sherry; combine well. Spoon into jars. Chill thoroughly. Add remaining strawberries on top in each jar and whipped cream, if desired. Store leftovers in refrigerator.

Yield: 12 8-oz. glass jars.

# Black Forest Cheesecake

1 cup Oreo cookie crumbs
1 cup whipping cream
3 tablespoons granulated sugar
1 8 oz. pkg. cream cheese, softened
2 tablespoons cocoa
1 teaspoon vanilla
1 21-oz. can cherry pie filling

In each glass jar, put about 2 level tablespoons of Oreo crumbs into the bottom. Refrigerate jars until ready for use.

Using an electric mixer, mix whipping cream and sugar until soft peaks have formed; set aside.

In a large bowl, beat cream cheese on medium high until smooth. Add whipping cream mixture to cream cheese and beat until mixture is smooth. Beat in cocoa and vanilla.

Remove jars from refrigerator. Top cookie crumbs with cheesecake batter, then a layer of pie filling (using about half the can), then another layer of cookie crumbs, cream cheese mixture and cherry pie filling. Add any leftover cookie crumbs to the top. Refrigerator for at least 1 hour before serving.

Yield: 4 8-oz. jars.

# Chocolate Nut Crunch

1 cup slivered almonds
1 cup plus 1 tablespoon butter, divided
Salt to taste
4 cups confectioners' sugar
1 cup cocoa
4 eggs
2 teaspoons vanilla
1 1/3 cups graham cracker crumbs
Kiwi or berries, optional

Spray jars with non-stick cooking spray. Sauté almonds in 1 tablespoon butter until lightly browned. Salt generously, taking care not to over-salt.

In a large bowl, combine sugar, cocoa, softened 1 cup butter, eggs and vanilla. Beat until smooth. In glass jars, spoon half the graham cracker crumbs, then add the cocoa mixture on top. Sprinkle almonds over top. Layer remaining graham cracker crumbs over all. Add kiwi or berries if desired. Refrigerate until served.

Yield: 10 8-oz. glass jars.

# Chocolate-Raspberry Parfaits

1 1/4 cups soy milk, chocolate flavored
3 1/2 oz. pkg. instant chocolate pudding mix
1/4 teaspoon cinnamon
1" thick slice of angel food cake
1/2 cup frozen fat-free whipped topping, thawed
1/2 cup frozen or fresh raspberries, thawed and drained

In a bowl, whisk soy milk, pudding mix and cinnamon with wire whisk until mixture thickens. To each of the 4 glass jars, add 2 tablespoons pudding mixture.

Add on top of the pudding mixture to each jar in this order:

1/4 of the angel food cake, torn into pieces
1 tablespoon whipped topping
2 tablespoons raspberries

Then add the rest of the pudding mixture and whipped topping.

Yield: 4 8-oz. glass jars.

# Low-Cal Orange Mousse

1/2 cup water
1 envelope unflavored gelatin
1/3 cup granulated sugar
1/4 cup frozen orange juice concentrate, thawed
1 cup plain low-fat yogurt
1 envelope (1.3 ounces) nondairy whipped topping mix
1/2 cup cold milk

In a small saucepan over low heat, add water and sprinkle with gelatin. Stirring often, bring to a simmer. Cook for about a minute or until the gelatin dissolves, stirring constantly. Stir in sugar, orange juice concentrate, and yogurt, then place pan in a large bowl of ice water. Stir until the mixture begins to mound - about 15 minutes.

Whip the topping and milk together until mixture forms soft peaks. Fold into the gelatin mixture. Spoon into glass jars and chill 3 hours.

Yield: 4 8-oz. glass jars.

# Orange Strawberry Dessert

1 pint ripe strawberries, hulled and halved
1 medium navel orange, peeled, halved, and cut in pieces
2 tablespoons grape juice
2 tablespoons orange juice
3 teaspoons granulated sugar

In a bowl, mix the strawberries and oranges together. Combine the grape juice and orange juice; drizzle over the fruit and mix well. Check to see if the strawberries are sweet enough and if not, add sugar. Put mixture in glass jars and refrigerate for 2 hours before serving.

Yield: 2 8-oz. glass jars.

# Whipped Pumpkin Cream Pie

2 cups milk
2 (3.5 oz.) boxes instant vanilla pudding
1 cup pumpkin
1 cup frozen whipped topping, thawed (Make whipping cream or use Cool Whip)
1 teaspoon pumpkin pie spice

*Graham Cracker Crust:*

1 1/2 cups graham cracker crumbs
1/3 cup granulated sugar
6 tablespoons butter, melted

In a small bowl, stir together the graham cracker crumbs and sugar. Add butter and mix well. Press about 4 level tablespoons of mixture into the bottom of each jar. Refrigerate jars until ready for use.

In a bowl, mix together milk, pudding, pumpkin, whipped topping and pumpkin pie spice. With a mixer, beat on low speed for 1 minute. Remove jars from refrigerator. Spoon the pumpkin mixture into the jars on top of the graham cracker crust.

Make the Spiced Whipped Cream below and add on top of pumpkin mixture. Refrigerate for 3 hours or until set.

Yield: 12 8 oz. jars.


*Spiced Whipped Cream:*

1/2 cup heavy whipping cream
1 tablespoon confectioners' sugar
1/2 teaspoon vanilla extract
1/2 teaspoon ground cinnamon

Chill the beaters and a mixing bowl in freezer for about 10 minutes. Beat whipping cream until thickened; beat in sugar, vanilla and cinnamon. Beat until soft peaks form; then beat about 2 minutes longer until stiff peaks form.

Yield: 1 cup.

# Mocha Pudding in Jars

1/3 cup granulated sugar
2 tablespoons cornstarch
1 tablespoon instant coffee granules
1/8 teaspoon salt
2 cups 1% low-fat milk
1/4 cup semisweet chocolate mini-chips
1 large egg yolk, beaten
1 teaspoon vanilla extract

In a medium saucepan, combine sugar, cornstarch, instant coffee and salt. Slowly add milk, stirring with a whisk until mixed. Stir in chocolate. Over medium heat, bring to a boil, stirring constantly. (about 7 minutes) Reduce heat and simmer 1 minute, stirring constantly. Stir a few tablespoons of hot mixture into egg yolk; add to remaining hot mixture. Cook 2 minutes, stirring constantly Remove from heat, and add vanilla. Pour into glass jars; cover with jar lids. Chill until set.

Yield: 4 8-oz. glass jars.

# Chocolate Layer Dessert

*Crust:*

1 cup all-purpose flour
1/2 cup margarine or butter, melted
1/2 cup nuts, chopped

*Filling:*

1 cup confectioners' sugar
1 8 oz. pkg. cream cheese
1 8 oz. pkg. frozen whipped dessert topping, thawed
1 large pkg. instant chocolate pudding
Extra chopped nuts for topping

Mix the flour, melted butter and nuts together. Sprinkle the mixture evenly in each glass jar. Bake at 350 degrees for 10 minutes.

In a medium bowl, beat together confectioners' sugar and cream cheese. Add 1/2 of the whipped dessert topping. Add the cream cheese mixture to the jars on top of the baked crust. Prepare the instant chocolate pudding as directed on box. Add to jars over the cream cheese mixture. Top this with the remaining 1/2 package of whipped dessert topping and sprinkle with chopped nuts.

Yield: 12 8-oz. glass jars.

# Chocolate Banana Crunch Parfait

3/4 cup skim milk
1 1.6 oz. pkg. chocolate sugar-free instant pudding mix
1 8 oz. container nonfat vanilla yogurt
1 envelope reduced-calorie whipped topping mix, prepared as directed on box
2 small ripe bananas, sliced
2 tablespoons toasted wheat germ

In medium bowl, combine milk, pudding mix and yogurt; blend well. Beat with wire whisk or hand mixer for 2 minutes or until creamy and smooth. Reserve 1/3 cup whipped topping for garnish; fold remaining whipped topping into pudding mix. Toss banana slices with wheat germ. Reserve 8 coated slices.

In each of eight glass jars, layer 3 tablespoons chocolate mixture, 1/8 of banana slices and another 3 tablespoons chocolate mixture. Top with a scant tablespoon of whipped topping and garnish with reserved banana slice. Serve immediately.

Yield: 8 8-oz. glass jars.

# Holiday Eggnog Dessert

1 package lemon jello
1 cup hot water
1 pint vanilla ice cream
1/4 teaspoon rum flavoring
1/4 teaspoon nutmeg
2 egg yolks, beaten
2 egg whites, stiffly beaten
1 cup heavy cream, whipped

*Graham Cracker Crust:*

3/4 cup graham cracker crumbs
2 tablespoons and 2 teaspoons packed brown sugar
3 tablespoons butter, melted

In a small bowl, stir together the graham cracker crumbs and sugar. Add butter and mix well. Spoon about 2 level tablespoons of mixture into the bottom of each jar.

Dissolve jello in hot water. Cut the ice cream into 8 chunks and add to jello; stir until ice cream melts. Refrigerate until jello is partially set. Add rum flavoring and nutmeg. Stir in egg yolks. Fold in egg whites.

Pour into glass jars on top of graham cracker crumbs. Top with whipped cream. Sprinkle nutmeg on top of whipped cream. Keep refrigerated until ready to serve.

Yield: 4 8-oz. jars.

# No Bake Pumpkin Pie

2 cups milk
2 3.4 oz. boxes instant vanilla pudding
1 cup canned pure pumpkin
1 cup frozen whipped dessert topping, thawed
1 teaspoon pumpkin pie spice

*Graham Cracker Crust:*

3/4 cup graham cracker crumbs
2 tablespoons and 2 teaspoons packed brown sugar
3 tablespoons butter, melted

In a small bowl, stir together the graham cracker crumbs and sugar. Add butter and mix well. Spoon about 2 level tablespoons of mixture into the bottom of each jar.

Mix milk, pudding, pumpkin, dessert topping and pumpkin pie spice together. Pour into jars on top of graham cracker crust. Refrigerate for 3 hours.

Yield: 10 8-oz. glass jars.

# GLAZES

After removing jar cakes from oven, poke holes in cakes with a fork, then pour the warm glaze over cakes. Cover the jars with their 2-part vacuum caps consisting of the gasket-lined metal lid and metal screw band. Screw lids on tightly. Within 15 to 20 minutes, the canning jars will begin to pop, creating an airtight vacuum.

## Butterscotch Cinnamon Glaze

2/3 cup butterscotch flavored chips
2 tablespoons heavy cream
2 tablespoons butter
1/8 teaspoon nutmeg
1/8 teaspoon cinnamon

In medium saucepan, combine butterscotch chips, heavy cream, butter, nutmeg and cinnamon. Cook in a heavy saucepan over medium heat, stirring constantly, until chips are melted and glaze is smooth.

Yield: 1/2 cup.

# Chocolate Almond Glaze

2/3 cup semi-sweet chocolate chips
1/3 cup heavy cream
1/4 cup butter
1 cup confectioners' sugar
1 teaspoon almond extract

In a saucepan, combine chocolate chips, cream and butter. Cook over medium heat, stirring constantly, until chips are melted and glaze is smooth. Pour glaze in a bowl and let cool for 10 minutes. Add confectioners' sugar and almond extract; mix well.

Yield: 2/3 cup.

# Milk Glaze

2 cups confectioners' sugar
3 tablespoons hot milk
2 teaspoons vanilla

Combine all the ingredients and blend until smooth.

Yield: 2/3 cup.

# Vanilla Glaze

1 tablespoon butter
1/2 teaspoon vanilla
2 1/2 tablespoons milk
1 1/2 cups confectioners' sugar
1/8 teaspoon salt

In a saucepan, melt the butter on low heat. Remove from heat, add vanilla and milk; stir. Add the confectioners' sugar and salt; blend until smooth. The glaze should be liquid but quite thick. If you want to thin it, add a little more milk.

Yield: 1/2 cup.

# Rum Glaze

2 1/2 cups confectioners' sugar
1/2 cup light rum
2 teaspoons vanilla

Mix the ingredients together until smooth. If the glaze seems too thick for easy spreading, add another teaspoon or two of rum or water.

Yield: 1 1/4 cups.

# Chocolate Glaze

1 tablespoon butter
1 square (1 oz.) unsweetened chocolate
1 cup confectioners' sugar
1 tablespoon milk
1 tablespoon water
1/2 teaspoon vanilla

Melt the butter and chocolate in a heavy saucepan over very low heat. Remove from heat. Add 1/3 cup of the confectioners' sugar and stir. In a cup, stir together the milk, water and vanilla. Add milk mixture and the remaining confectioners' sugar to the chocolate mixture and stir. Blend all the ingredients with a wire whisk until very smooth. If you want to thin it, add a little more water.

Yield: 1/2 cup.

# Lemon Glaze

1/4 cup lemon juice
1 teaspoon vanilla
1 1/4 cups confectioners' sugar

Stir the ingredients together and blend until smooth.

Yield: 3/4 cup.

# Mocha Glaze

2 squares (2 oz.) unsweetened chocolate
2 tablespoons butter
1 1/3 cups confectioners' sugar
1/8 teaspoon salt
4 tablespoons hot coffee
1/2 teaspoon vanilla

Melt the chocolate and butter in a heavy saucepan over low heat, stirring constantly. In a bowl, stir together the confectioners' sugar, salt, coffee and vanilla. Add the chocolate mixture to the sugar mixture and beat until smooth. If necessary, thin the glaze with a little more coffee.

Yield: 3/4 cup.

# Butterscotch Cream Cheese Frosting

2/3 cup butterscotch flavored morsels
1 8-oz. package cream cheese, softened
1/4 cup butter, softened
2 1/2 cups sifted confectioners' sugar
1 tablespoon lemon juice

Melt over hot (not boiling) water, butterscotch flavored morsels; stir until smooth. Set aside. In large bowl, combine cream cheese and butter; beat until creamy. Gradually add confectioners' sugar and lemon juice; beat well Blend in melted morsels; chill 15 minutes before frosting cake. Excellent on carrot or applesauce cake; try it on any of the cakes in jars. Keep frosted cake refrigerated until ready to serve.

Yield: 1 1/2 cups.

Exclusively for *Desserts In Jars* readers:

# Over 600 Online Labels for the desserts in this book - Available at

www.InJars.com

Hey, if you loved this book and want to get more freebies and recipes like these, subscribe to the newsletter at:

http://www.BonnieScottAuthor.com/subscribe.html

Also by Bonnie Scott

  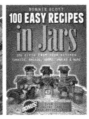  

Cookie Indulgence – 150 Easy Cookie Recipes

4 Ingredient Cookbook: 150 Quick Timesaving Recipes

Chocolate Bliss

100 Easy Camping Recipes

View more of my books at my Amazon Author Page

https://www.amazon.com/Bonnie-Scott/e/B008MM40AY

*All titles available in Paperback and Kindle versions at Amazon.com*

Made in United States
North Haven, CT
21 March 2022

17387453R00254